A DEATH OF ONE'S OWN

BY GERDA LERNER

SIMON AND SCHUSTER   NEW YORK

PUBLISHED BY SIMON AND SCHUSTER
A DIVISION OF GULF & WESTERN CORPORATION
SIMON & SCHUSTER BUILDING
ROCKEFELLER CENTER
1230 AVENUE OF THE AMERICAS
NEW YORK, NEW YORK 10020

DESIGNED BY EVE METZ
MANUFACTURED IN THE UNITED STATES OF AMERICA

1   2   3   4   5   6   7   8   9   10

LIBRARY OF CONGRESS CATALOGING IN PUBLICATION DATA

LERNER, GERDA, DATE.
    A DEATH OF ONE'S OWN.

    1. BRAIN—TUMORS—BIOGRAPHY.   2. LERNER,   GERDA,   1920–
    I. TITLE.
RC280.B7L48   616.9'94'810926 [B]   78-45
ISBN 0-671-24008-0

The author wishes to thank Howard Nemerov for permission to reprint his poem "The Common Wisdom," from American Poetry Review *May–June, 1975, and also collected in* The Western Approaches *by Howard Nemerov,* © 1975 The University of Chicago Press.

TO CARL

for the last time and always—

the love we shared
the marriage we made
our friendship

This book is a fragment made up of fragments. It is a figment of the imagination, a distorted aspect of a larger whole. Distorted by subjectivity and pain, distorted by shame, even though I have struggled against it, distorted most of all by my limited vision. It is, in short, nothing else than all works of art: experience filtered through the mind and feelings of one subject-object-agent. It differs from literature in that the events happened "actually," and that the names and the characters of the principals are real. That seems, even as I write it, an odd statement, for the way I see it now the distinctions between the actual, the imaginary and the mythical are much more tenuous than I had understood earlier. I can describe what I recall happened during a particular day, a particular hour, but my memory is tricky and distorts. My diary notes of that day read very differently from the recalled event, and so I have included my diary notes. The poems occasioned by the same event and designed to contain it and possibly control it by magic and craft read differently still—and so I have included the poems. Perhaps all of it will add up to another sort of truth: layered, organic, functional.

Nothing I have written here can resurrect a moment of Carl Lerner's life nor recapture the essentials of his character: that rare combination of gentleness and strength, the loyalty and goodness, the fastidious craftsmanship, the adventuresome creativity. Nothing here can do justice to the achievement and meaning of our thirty-three years of joint experience. The simple statement that for this long a time ours was a happy, deeply satisfying marriage seems somewhat suspect, even preposterous. That it was a marriage which allowed for the

7

growth of each of us and in which each supplied for the other the steady trust necessary for such growth will have meaning only to those who have experienced a similar relationship; to the others such words will have no concreteness.

I have not attempted to render these intangibles. When I began this work, I wanted to record the death of a man, a fine and dearly beloved man, and its meaning to those near him. That was my intent, but it soon became clear that this was too difficult a task. No one knows the experience of the dying. Even the most sympathetic observation can capture only its paltry outward manifestations. So what this has become is an account of my own experience with death, with the deaths of those I have loved, with this one very special and overwhelming death.

Carl had the finely observant eye of the filmmaker, the ability to participate in an event and yet to see it at a distance, the urge to experience and then to shape the experience into a work of art. He would understand what I have attempted to do: not merely to ease my pain and find my own way back into life, but to record and perhaps thereby give larger meaning to this final portion of our joint experience. Carl shaped his own death as surely as he shaped his life and there is no need to attempt to interpret it. Nor is this intended to be a memorial; this would run counter to the way he lived his life and to the way he regarded his own death as something natural, organic, inevitable.

What I hope for is to banish and conquer fear: my own fear and terror of the unknowable and irrational, of uncontrollable random disaster. Implicitly, also, the fear all of us share as we try to avoid dealing with death, as we ritualize it and try to minimize its impact on our lives.

In the writing I imposed upon myself a demand for the kind of ruthless honesty in facing myself and my most personal feelings that one accepts in a psychoanalytic relationship, while admitting frankly the limitations of my perception of others. The names of most of the living have been altered and that seems like a thin disguise. There is one deliberate omission: I have left out of this narrative everything essential pertaining to my children and their relationship to the event of their father dying. I have done this because I do not feel I know what their experience really was nor do I feel that I could describe my perception of it without invading their privacy and possibly causing them pain. This I have chosen not to do.

I have tried to look straight at death and to let myself experience it fully. To know it, feel it . . . Dying is part of living, part of my life, part of my reentry. Acceptance of death is the key to life.

March–April 25, 1972

Who, nowadays, cares for a well-crafted death? No-
body. . . . It is rare to find anyone who wishes to
have a death of his own . . . I think it must have
been different in the old days. Long ago they knew
(or perhaps they perceived dimly) that one carried
death within oneself the way the fruit carries the
pit within itself. The children had a small one in-
side and the grown-ups a big one. The women car-
ried it in their wombs and the men in their chest.
One possessed *it and there was a peculiar dignity*
and a quiet pride in that possession. . . .

Rainer Maria Rilke,
The Notebooks of Malte Laurids Brigge

It had been a rather bad season for us. In July 1971 our daughter Stephanie was the victim of a traffic accident in New Delhi and suffered a severe concussion and triple skull fractures. We spent a horrible month in India nursing her and trying to persuade her to return to the United States for further tests and treatment. She recovered quite well, but refused to return home. On our return to New York Carl had a previously scheduled surgery in the hope of restoring his hearing, which in one ear was minimal and not too good in the other. The surgery, by itself uneventful, failed, and there was no further means of arresting the slow deterioration of his hearing. We worried a good deal over the implications of this disability. Carl's lifework was film editing, a work in which hearing was nearly as important as sight.

I felt he should turn to full-time college teaching of film editing and production, something he was now doing on a part-time basis, and gradually retire from the film industry. He disagreed quite vehemently. Filmmaking was his work, he said, not teaching, which was fine, but incidental to his real vocation. Being a teacher myself and knowing how successful and sought after he was as a teacher, I thought his decision wrong and said so. But once his mind was made up, he could not be budged. He would stop making films when he no longer could make films, no sooner.

I was sick on our return with an old complaint, which the tensions and stress of the summer had aggravated, By December, major surgery could no longer be put off. In order to miss only two weeks from my work, I arranged to have the surgery during the college Christmas vacation and then take two weeks' leave in January for recuperation time. Everything went as planned, except that I was seriously anemic after the surgery. With my recovery slower than I had anticipated, it took me to the beginning of February to regain my strength. It had been quite a winter. . . . The fact that there was war in India and that Stephanie traveled and lived very near the war zone did not help matters. We were without news from her for months and we worried. By February, the India-Pakistan war had stopped; Stephanie was safely in Europe; I was feeling like myself again. We decided to reward ourselves for the trials and tribulations of the past six months by taking a two-week Caribbean vacation during my March intersession.

When he heard we were going to Nassau, where he has a friend he wanted to visit, our son Daniel decided to join us. We were very pleased. It was the first time since he had left home for college that he joined us for a vacation. Daniel was then twenty-five, living in Philadelphia. He was a free-lance cameraman, doing well and living a life quite independent from ours. We were on very good terms and saw each other at least once a month. But brief visits, in our busy lives, were very different from having two relaxed vacation weeks together. We all looked forward to the trip.

It turned out to be a wonderful vacation. Danny had arrived a day earlier than we did and met us at the airport. We stayed at a quiet motel within three minutes' walk from the beach, but spent most of our days at the house of Danny's friend Susan on Paradise Island. As Danny's parents we were accepted into Susan's relaxed household, in which people drifted in and out, enjoyed the magnificent beach, the casual hospitality, the comfort and luxury Susan so generously shared. The young people were only mildly interested in us and that suited us fine. Carl and I spent much time lying lazily on the beach and some time playing silly games with Susan's beautiful four-year-old boy. There was always someone ready to cook a fabulous feast of local fish and seafood. There were long slow walks on the clean white sand. Sometimes, Danny sat with us and talked; sometimes, he brought over one of the local girls he had met. There was nothing special about this vacation except that it was good, very relaxed, and that it was our last one. If one could choose a last vacation after a long life together this was the kind to choose, but life does not work that way and we did not know anything and for this I am grateful. After those days, I knew too much all the time and it seems to me now there will never again be a time as carefree and easy and full of joy as those last days in Nassau.

Carl was in fine physical shape; he was lean, marvelously tanned, radiantly healthy. Nearly sixty, he had not felt or looked younger in a decade. The same cannot be said for me. I was still feeling the effects of the surgery, of the tensions and worries of the past ten months. But the sun, the clean blue water, the pleasant sights of the island, had a curative effect. We swam for hours, stretched out in deck chairs, holding a book, but too lazy to read it. We drank rich rum drinks, which made us giddy and silly. It is hard for me to remember what we talked about as we sat by the beach in the warm nights, watching the stars in the clear sky.

We went gambling once. We took a tour of the island. We walked through the straw market for hours, trying on this hat or that, buying ugly crocheted bags and useless, brightly colored table mats. We watched the luxury cruise ships pull into the harbor and we talked about the trips we meant to take in the future: one to South America, one to Mexico, places where we'd never been.

Daily, in our bathing suits and beach shorts, we took the ferry boat which ran between Nassau harbor and Paradise Island. It was a dangerously overcrowded motorboat without life belts, which was run indifferently and capriciously by an old, potbellied man or one of his slick, bare-chested young nephews. It is ironic to remember that we used to worry about the safety of the ferry, speculating what would happen if it got swamped. The second week of our vacation I noticed a slight peculiarity in the way Carl fished for the coins in his bathing trunk pocket to pay the fare. He seemed clumsy, taking a long time to get the change out while the young man who collected the money impatiently tapped his foot. The next day, the same thing happened. The third day, Carl dropped the coins after fishing them out. On the return trip he fumbled again and I reached into his pocket to get them. We talked about there being something wrong with the pocket or the way he was sitting. Carl noticed that the fourth and fifth fingers of his right hand seemed slightly stiff in the joint, which was why he had trouble with the coins. On the following day I carried the change.

We began to observe this stiffness of his fingers on other occasions. We decided it was his arthritis acting up. He had been troubled with arthritis in the neck and right shoulder for years and had a long history of fruitlessly seeking medical help for the pain which at times was so severe he could not sleep. The previous summer we had gone to a European clinic specializing in such cases. After four weeks of treatment the orthopedist had told Carl that there was an arthritic spur pressing against a nerve and that he well might expect the pain and discomfort to continue and even to spread. There was little that could be done for it, until it got worse and hurt his arm, when surgery might be indicated. Quite logically, we thought of this prediction and briefly worried about it.

I remember that morning quite vividly. We all went once more to Paradise Island, leaving early since Danny had to return to the States for a job he was shooting over the weekend. I swam perhaps a mile from one end of the island to the place where we usually sat; Carl walked alongside me on the beach. I remember floating on my back and looking at him as he walked along, thinking how well he looked, how handsome he was after all these years. When I joined him and we both stretched out side by side on the beach chairs, I sensed his mood had changed. He was depressed and somber. I did not have to ask what was the matter. He kept rubbing his fingers. The joints were slightly crooked.

"You're worried?" I asked.

"What do you think? It's gotten worse."

I explained once again about the arthritic spur pressing on the nerve. Perhaps when we got home he would have to wear a neck collar for a while to relieve the pressure. He had no pain in the finger, did he?

"No."

"Listen, you." I sat on his chair and put my face very close to his, looking into his eyes. "Keep your pecker up, will you? Promise me? It's just your arthritis."

We were both thinking of the possibility of surgery. No need to say so; we were on the same wavelength. "It's disagreeable," I said, "but maybe this will finally make you get the medical treatment you need." We had for years been quarreling about his neglecting his health.

Danny came over to us and we all returned to Nassau so he could pack and leave. As he and I waited outside for his cab, Danny did a strange thing. Handing me a piece of paper with an address on it, he made a little speech. "Listen, Mom, I can't explain why, but I'm worried about this thing with Daddy's fingers. I asked this girl I met here for the name of a good doctor on the island and I also asked Susan, and here are the names. I want you to promise me to take Daddy to the doctor tomorrow. If necessary, come home a couple of days sooner."

I laughed about his anxiety and assured him there was no need to rush home, since we knew what we were dealing with and it was a chronic condition.

"Well, anyway," he said. "Just in case."

Such concern was unusual for him and Carl and I were both touched by it. Sufficiently so to make a halfhearted attempt to contact the local doctors. But it was the Easter weekend and neither of them was working. We drove to the hospital, took one look at the crowded emergency waiting room and dismissed the idea. Carl absolutely refused to leave for New York earlier than Tuesday, as we had planned. The whole trouble was so minor, it seemed silly even to have gone through all these steps. We decided to forget about it and enjoy the four days remaining of our vacation. And we did.

Once on the plane to New York, Carl expressed a sense of urgency about seeing a doctor. It seemed to him the fingers were stiffer than they had been. We discussed whom to see. I thought he should see an orthopedist, but he had little confidence in the two men he had seen for his shoulder. We decided to call two friends, who were doctors, and get their recommendation. We did it that night, on arrival.

Both doctors questioned me about his symptoms. Did he have pain? Dizziness? Any other complaints? One advised him to stay in bed or at least move as little as possible. The other thought that was not necessary, but cautioned him not to use his right arm at all. Each recommended an orthopedist.

Their reaction alarmed me. It appeared obvious they suspected spinal injury and wanted to guard him against further complications. I decided to call a close friend, an eye surgeon, whose medical judgment we greatly respected. He considered the matter, having asked similar questions as the other doctors, and advised us to consult not an orthopedist but an internist. He explained that this was likely to be a diagnostic problem. Given the United States health-care system, it was best in such cases to have an internist who could coordinate the whole diagnostic procedure rather than try to find the best specialist on one's own. First-rate medical work must be done as teamwork and no layman knows how to select such a team. He gave us the name of his own internist, but warned us not to be annoyed if the man could not see Carl for several days. He was a very busy specialist.

This piece of advice was excellent and I shall always be grateful for it. Without it we never would have found the superb team of doctors and the fine hospital we did find, nor would we have gotten the immediate attention which was needed. We might have wandered from one specialist to another for weeks.

Instead, when Carl called the internist, Dr. Wolbrenner, the next morning, he was asked to come in immediately. After a brief examination, Dr. Wolbrenner agreed that Carl indeed represented a diagnostic problem. He wanted a neurosurgeon to see him that day. The man he suggested, Dr. Ambrose, saw him that afternoon and confirmed the internist's verdict that he needed a series of diagnostic tests. He spoke of the possibility of pressure on the spine, pressure on the nerve, the need for being under close observation, possibly under traction. It might, he explained, take several days to get a hospital room. Meanwhile Carl should remain quietly at home, avoiding all strain.

Carl accepted it all with admirable composure. He seemed rather pleased at the speedy attention he had received and felt himself to be in good hands. He was always quite naive in medical matters. While I encouraged his confidence for the time being, I was very alarmed. Obviously, only suspicions of the very worst kind could induce two busy specialists to see at once a patient they had never seen before and to hospitalize him instantly. I thought of the immediate reaction of our doctor friends and it added up to the fact that they knew something we did not. I guessed it was disk trouble in the cervical spine. Spinal surgery—a really alarming prospect.

Two days later Carl was in a lovely private room, overlooking the East River in one of New York City's great teaching hospitals. He was in fine spirits, pleased with the battery of tests he had been given and with the obvious expertise of his team of doctors. The three fingers of his right hand were a little more crooked and stiff than they had been on our return from Nassau. But we felt more confident—we would know the answer in a few days.

Dr. Wolbrenner was at his finest during this period. He selected the specialists, briefed us on their findings and interpreted their opinions. It seemed, a few days later, that the experts wanted to look "a little higher up," just to make sure. They had begun to put Carl's neck into traction for several hours a day, in the hope that this might relieve the pressure on the nerve. Apparently, that did not happen, for by now the entire hand was stiff. Skull X rays and brain scan were negative.

After a thorough neurological examination which was performed by a young whiz kid, Dr. David Goldman, whom both Doctors Ambrose and Wolbrenner had praised extravagantly as "the brightest young man on the staff," he had some concrete information for us: we were not dealing with a problem of spinal pressure on the nerve. Had there been such pressure, the stiff fingers would have been associated with severe neck pain. We were dealing with a problem originating in the brain.

When I heard this I understood why all the doctors had acted with such urgency from the start. The moment we reported paralysis without pain, they knew we were most likely dealing with a lesion in the brain.

Dr. Goldman assured us that they had not entirely given up on the possibility of spinal involvement. He himself felt certain the problem was "higher up." Tests would have to continue and be repeated. Meanwhile, physical therapy to the hand was started.

By now our medical team consisted of an internist, a neurosurgeon, two neurologists, an orthopedist, a physical rehabilitation specialist. After a second brain scan they told us they were highly suspicious of pressure in the brain but could not, so far, locate it. They proposed close observation for a week, daily checks, then a repetition of the brain scan. If necessary there were more sophisticated tests, but it was best to wait with these. The main thing was to see what happened with the hand.

The hand got stiffer, but not totally immobile. After a week, Carl had no grasp left at all, but could move the fingers. He was now very anxious to get a definite diagnosis. He talked about spinal surgery with a sort of fatalism—anything was better than losing the use of his right hand. His livelihood depended on his right hand; everything depended on his right hand.

During this first week in the hospital Carl established a reputation as a very special sort of patient, a very special sort of person. He always had a gift with people; he was charming, gentle, considerate. His reputation as a film artist spread around the ward; nurses, orderlies, technicians came in to look on him as a minor celebrity and went away charmed by his modesty, openness and steady good humor. We also established a relationship with the doctors, at least with those who would be the "main" doctors. From the start, we insisted on being involved in the medical search, the medical decisions and on being told the truth at every stage. This was considered highly unusual. It became more unusual as the case progressed.

April 19

After 14 days in the hospital, the hand is worse. The latest brain scan shows a shadow. The doctors are now convinced there is a mass of some sort. In order

to tell what kind and to locate it exactly, a cerebral angiogram has to be done. It is a procedure involving the
main artery to the brain and it is done under local anesthesia. There is a 1% risk of complication. What kind of
complication? Well, paralysis or sometimes death. But a
1% risk isn't a very great risk. What is the risk of not
doing the angiogram? If there should be a tumor and it
is not found in time, the risk can be very great indeed.
In fact, the doctors considered the angiogram absolutely
essential.

By then, the idea of a brain tumor had been around
long enough for us to get accustomed to it. The ward
was full of patients who had been operated on for brain
tumors and were making recoveries. They were, of
course, all terribly unfortunate patients, very much
more complicated cases, which was what accounted for
their sorry state. We did not much like looking at them;
they were quite an upsetting group and so we kept to
the room a lot. But we did know several people who had
made perfectly good recoveries from brain tumors. We
also knew one, a very close friend, who had died of a
brain tumor. We thought she had died a terrible death,
and during those days we never mentioned her name.
We were progressing rather quickly. Typically, Carl cut
right through the whole discussion about the angiogram. There was no question in his mind he would have
it done. As soon as possible. His hand had to be saved,
that was all there was to it.

April 20

The angiogram was done early in the morning
and it went well. No complications. Carl made a comfortable recovery. We were told there would be no results
until the "reading" tomorrow.

April 21

The news was bad. There definitely was a mass
on the angiogram, indicating a brain tumor. It was im-

possible to tell what kind without surgery. Unfortu-
nately the mass was in a fairly inaccessible region. That
is, it was located on the left side of the brain, just above
the motor center and near the center that controls
speech, so that even exploratory surgery involved the risk
of damaging motor activity and speech. Spreading paral-
ysis, in other words. Brain tumors were of various kinds,
some of the benign ones simply encapsulated themselves
and stayed as they were for long periods of time, even
years. Possibly this was of such a kind, in which case one
might hope to improve the hand by physical therapy. On
the other hand, if it were malignant, it would grow and
the symptoms would worsen. The best thing would be to
send Carl home and have a few weeks of observation,
while physical therapy continued.

I spoke to Dr. Ambrose and Dr. Wolbrenner outside
the room. How serious did they think it was? They repeated what they had said. It really was impossible to
tell. But the reason they could not operate now was that
such surgery almost certainly would involve paralysis of
the right arm, possibly the right leg—which might be
permanent. It was certainly not wise to do it while his
complaint was so relatively minor. "Minor," I said. "His
hand is paralyzed. He can't work. You don't understand—for a creative person like him, this is the very
worst thing—"

They were very kind about it. In certain situations
conservative treatment was the wisest thing. We would
know more in a few weeks, without doubt. It was hard,
they could appreciate our anxiety, but the location of
the mass . . . It appeared, after all, that it was I who did
not yet understand. I was still worried about his hand
and nothing else.

April 22, Saturday

Discharge from the hospital. That is always a
joyous moment, no matter how upsetting the situation.
Dr. Ambrose gave Carl an appointment for Tuesday

morning, told him to follow his usual routine, but avoid fatigue. He hoped for the best.

When we got home, Carl was very tired. Naturally, after all the tension and excitement . . . He took a nap, then friends called. We watched TV after dinner. Carl seemed uneasy and nervous all evening. Finally, just before we went to bed, he told me he felt his wrist was getting stiff. I examined it and could not verify it, I reassured him—probably it was just fatigue. He hoped so, and we went to sleep.

The next morning, the wrist was definitely not as mobile as it had been. I called Dr. Ambrose and he said to bring Carl to his office Monday morning, instead of Tuesday. It might very well be from the strain of the trip.

We took a stroll outdoors, enjoying the sunshine and the freedom of walking. Later friends came to visit; Carl chatted and laughed with them and seemed to be having a good time. But after they left, his face changed at once. He was tense and grim. "It's up to the elbow," he said.

The hand was stiff, the wrist was stiffening. He had slightly impaired mobility in the elbow, but he could flex it. "Something's happening," he said.

I cannot recall the moment; I cannot recall the words we said. But we both felt what we would feel for so long: a sense of helpless entrapment, a bewildered dread.

Later, we talked about the doctors, the hospital. We felt lucky to have been in that place. We had enormous confidence in Dr. Ambrose, a sensitive man of extraordinary humanity and patience.

That night something began that would become a pattern of conduct between us; although we never spoke of it we fell into it automatically. We never tried for false cheerfulness, for comforting words, and we never indulged in self-pity. We didn't say don't worry or words of comfort or words of hope. We went to bed and we knew we were in trouble and we might just as well let it sink in and find a way of floating with it. We held each other close; as always I was on his left side and he had his arm around me as we went to sleep and that was comfort enough.

The next morning it was still dark when I woke up from an uncomfortable feeling that Carl was awake next to me. I turned toward him. His eyes were wide open and still and there was a terrible look on his face. He waited an instant until he saw I was really awake and the thought flashed through my mind, He's been like this for some time, why didn't he wake me? Then he said, very softly, "My arm is gone."

He could not lift his right arm. The entire arm from the shoulder to the fingers was paralyzed.

We tested the rest of his body. Everything else was all right.

"We've got to get you back to the hospital."

"Yes."

This was it. I wasn't thinking about anything except the practical questions. It was 6:00 A.M. It would take me at least a half hour to get dressed and get Carl dressed. I decided to let the doctor sleep another half hour, and got us ready. It was terrible to move his dead arm around. I was afraid to hurt it, but Carl wanted it moved and fast. He helped with his good hand. We got his shirt on. He was determined and angry. Eager to get going, get to the hospital.

Dr. Ambrose called back within five minutes. Get him to the emergency room, he said. I'll make the arrangements and meet you there. "All right to take him by car?" Yes.

We were back at the hospital by 7:30 A.M.

That day, for the first time, he was frantic. A steady procession of doctors, specialists, nurses, technicians, passed through the room, doing what they had to do. He pleaded, argued, railed at them. "Do something, will you! Operate—today! I can't just lie here waiting to become paralyzed limb by limb."

Dr. Ambrose had already told me they would have to operate. There was now no choice. The tumor was obviously spreading fast. The problem was operating room space. The operating room was solidly booked until Thursday.

At this, I too grew frantic. Thursday! By then his other arm might be paralyzed. His leg.

The fact was, Dr. Ambrose explained, that it was quite likely that after surgery both the right arm and the right leg would be paralyzed. He hoped this would be temporary. With some luck— Then followed a long technical explanation.

If there is no choice, then there is no choice. But waiting like this is too much to ask of human beings. . . .

Dr. Ambrose thought he could push Carl ahead for Wednesday surgery. Carl was not pacified. "You can't expect me to lie here and wait till I go piece by piece . . ." Usually self-controlled and reticent, he let his anger and despair surface freely that day. Rage is the psyche's first defense against overwhelming disaster. Fate is unfair and man finds unfairness of such magnitude incomprehensible. Why me? Why not another? Why now? These questions he never asked, but they were there. The futile explosion of rage was a poor substitute for action, but it was all we had.

Friends kept calling, but we let only a very few come to visit briefly. The hours dragged. Late in the afternoon Dr. Ambrose called and told Carl he had managed to schedule him for Tuesday at 5:00 P.M. This "good" news calmed him down. A definite time, even twenty-four hours away, was bearable.

I did not then know that brain surgery is always scheduled for early morning and that Dr. Ambrose was scheduled to do a six-hour procedure Tuesday morning. His willingness to schedule Carl after that surgery meant that he considered his condition very grave indeed. Anticipating this sort of surgery is somewhat like anticipating an execution. One tries hard not to make pictures in the mind. One tries to divert the patient. From habit, one eats lunch and supper. We watched TV. Read the paper. Cracked stupid jokes and avoided any heavy talk. It occurred to me he ought to be making decisions about the future. I agonized, unable to decide whether to call up our daughter in Holland and give her a chance to come home. In the end I forced myself to dismiss these plans as morbid and counterproductive. He would have a tumor removed tomorrow. For some weeks he would be very sick. Then he would recover. We played it that way.

We waited. Waiting of this kind is the most refined form of torture. I had convinced myself that the best I could do for Carl was just to be there and let him act and make all the decisions. If he was going to be brave about it and treat the whole situation by ignoring it, so would I.

In the evening friends came to visit, a psychoanalyst and his wife, who is a colleague of mine. We had worked together and had become friends and I had through her learned of some of the personal tragedies the two of them had suffered and survived with fortitude, honesty and good humor. There is a sort of self-selected fraternity of those suffering extreme disasters. You know that *they* know, since they've been through it, so you can cut through a lot of explaining, posturing and avoidance mechanisms. Carl, who was not as close to them as I was, sensed this and was very pleased by their visit, although he had that same evening refused to see some close old friends.

A few minutes later I had serious doubts about that decision. Our psychiatrist friend, after some innocuous conversation, asked Carl if he had been wondering about tomorrow's procedure. I signaled frantically with my eyes, but was ignored.

Carl said, with some eagerness, that of course he had.

"Well, what they do is they drill holes in your skull, using very fine precision tools, much like regular drills," our friend explained very matter-of-factly. "There are no nerves in the skull and this would be painless even without anesthesia."

If it had been anyone else I would have intervened by now. But, I told myself, the man is a doctor, he's also a psychiatrist. Maybe he knows what he's doing. Also, I looked at Carl's face. He was genuinely interested.

Then followed a lengthy technical explanation of brain surgery, interrupted once or twice by Carl's questions. He was fascinated and seemed gratified to have his questions answered honestly. I, too, found myself getting involved. Some of the science-fiction pictures, which I had been trying so hard to keep out of my mind, dissolved. Still, it seemed to me like risky business to talk that way. I started mumbling about Carl needing his rest.

"I'll just tell you one funny story," our friend said, "then we'll go." His wife smiled at me reassuringly. The story that followed was hardly reassuring.

A man went to the bar and asked for the usual. Bartender brought him a double martini. The man gulped it down and asked for another. Same routine. After the third round, the customer heaved a deep sigh. "Feeling better?" the bartender asked sympathetically. The man nodded. The bartender went on: "Had a hard day? How's the brain surgery going, Doc?" "Not bad," the man said.

I jumped up, really angry. But Carl was laughing uproariously, with real enjoyment, and before I knew it I was laughing, too. The sheer brass of it . . .

"Tough-minded," Carl said admiringly after our friends departed. "Good people for tough situations." I had to agree. We chuckled a few times more, recalling the conversation. The tone had been just right. In the months to come we would increasingly find sentimentality, pity or a tragic stance unbearable and ludicrous. We had, without knowing, shaped our attitude that day. Honesty, informed knowledge, good humor, open anger and, finally, tough-minded defiance. We would cultivate that in ourselves, demand it of those we depended on and project it to those of our friends who could bear it. We would stay with that to the end. Whatever saving grace there was, this was it.

Danny came in the afternoon. His presence cheered Carl greatly. These two had such an easy, openly affectionate relationship based on respect and mutual pride in each other. Father and son, they always seemed to me to have more in common naturally than I had with either. Now I noticed how Danny's reaction instinctively paralleled his father's. It felt good to know he was young and strong and would be with us in this.

Late in the evening, after surgery and evening rounds, Dr. Ambrose came into the room. He sat down, relaxed and unhurried, as though we were his only concern. The surgery was all set for tomorrow 5:00 P.M. He answered our questions, which were few, and expressed satisfaction that we had caught this thing in the early stages. So often people did not recognize they had trouble until it was very late. His tone was confident, encouraging, concerned.

Then he began asking Carl questions about his work. His questions were detailed and searching and got Carl talking with his usual inspired enthusiasm about film editing—the technique, the craft, the creative aspect. What he loved about filmmaking was the mixture of individual creativity and collective work. Every film project he had ever worked on was an organizing job, a battle over conflicting interests, a triumph of teamwork over personal ambition. If that teamwork could not be created, the venture failed. Carl talked about the great directors he had worked with—Sidney Lumet, William Friedkin, Alan Pakula. They all knew, in the final resort, how to blend the talents of the many creative people on the film into something new and whole—the work itself.

"Like a surgical team," Dr. Ambrose said.

Yes, or a symphony orchestra. Carl said he had been lucky—or perhaps it was more than luck, a matter of choice—to have worked on films which were serious works of art: *Twelve Angry Men; The Fugitive Kind; No Exit; On the Bowery; Come Back, Africa.* . . .

"That's remarkable," Dr. Ambrose said.

No, it was simply a matter of refusing work he did not consider—well, at least humanist in content. He had been offered *The Godfather* just recently and refused it, although he could tell it would be a surefire winner, Academy Awards and all that . . . Carl looked at me sideways and I grinned. Yeah, he had not even bothered to tell me about it until after he had refused, he had been that sure of his decision. We kept our professional lives independent from each other. "I didn't like the excessive violence in that picture," Carl said, "the glorification of violence. I consider that immoral. So the films I've worked on have been films I could believe in."

"That's what keeps surgeons going," Dr. Ambrose commented. "No matter how tough it sometimes is— you believe in what you are doing."

"I've sometimes wondered how you deal with failure."

"Scientifically first." Dr. Ambrose obviously had given the subject some thought. "You learn from failures. You try to analyze where you might improve. You experiment." He talked about his animal experiments, on which he was working constantly in hopes of improving his technique and knowledge. "But also, you accept human limitations. There are mysterious, irrational aspects to human existence. The body is not simply a machine which we can learn to understand mechanically. There is personality, the psyche—" The conversation went on like that, good talk, the kind intelligent people who have curiosity about one another have on a leisurely evening, on a holiday. I marveled at Dr. Ambrose's obvious personal involvement and at his generosity in giving us his time. I thought he was trying to reassure Carl and win his confidence, which he certainly succeeded in doing. When he left, the three of us felt we had been most fortunate in our choice of a surgeon. If anyone could be trusted, it was this man.

Outside the door of Carl's room, Dr. Ambrose told me he wanted to put on a night nurse—midnight to 8:00 A.M. shift. It was fairly routine to do this before surgery, just to make sure the patient got complete rest and could be comforted at once in case he was anxious. I agreed and asked if I might be permitted to stay past visiting hours until the nurse came.

Dr. Ambrose said he would ordinarily not give his permission, since relatives so often upset the patient. But he felt he had gotten to know us sufficiently to understand that my presence would help Carl. He wrote out an order giving me unlimited access to the room, not just for that night, but for the future.

I was very grateful for this gesture, both for its real value to us and for its symbolic meaning which indicated we were being treated as individuals, not just as patients. But my ignorance of what lay ahead made it impossible for me to understand that evening what a truly remarkable thing Dr. Ambrose had done in having his long talk with Carl. He already knew the kind of situation and decisions he would likely have to face the next day. Literally, life-and-death decisions, determining also the quality of life which was to be preserved, not just its length. Any surgeon would be justified in refusing to personalize such a decision. If one does not know the patient as a person, one can go simply by training and skill. A surgeon is not God and, by staying impersonal, his moral responsibility is more limited. Dr. Ambrose chose to go the other way. He made it his business to get to know the individual, his family, his life situation. Then, faced with his awesome decisions, he took the responsibility on the basis of informed judgment plus medical skill to help this particular individual. This takes enormous moral courage and it takes what Dr. Ambrose would so consistently project: humility and respect for the rights of patients. Even terminal patients.

In retrospect, passing through this hellish experience,

we had the good fortune to encounter some extraordinary human beings. That helped.

About 11:00 P.M. that evening, just as Carl was ready to settle down to sleep, the nurse told me he would be put in surgery at 7:00 A.M. the next morning. There had been a cancellation and they had moved him ahead. The resident would be down to "prep" him in a few minutes. We were exhilarated by this good fortune. Carl was so pleased he bore with infinite patience the clumsy attention of the fatigued and irritable resident, who at midnight took his history, did a few tests and shaved his head with what appeared to be a blunt paring knife.

Ghoulishly bald-headed and inordinately cheerful, Carl thanked him, dubbed him "The Butcher" to his departing back, kissed Danny and me with restraint and demanded we go home so he could have a decent night's sleep.

We did and he did and he went up for surgery at 6:30 A.M. on April 25, 1972. Danny and I came back to the hospital about eleven, prepared to wait.

The very competent Irish day supervisor of nurses scolded me for coming so early, gave me her office to rest in and fed me cups of coffee.

"By the way," I asked innocently, "how come you get cancellations on the neurosurgery floor?"

"We never do," she said. "We just move the less urgent cases down when we have a real emergency."

Her words sank into me like a lead weight. I had been told in many different ways and, certainly, I already knew. People have complex ways of dealing with painful knowledge. As long as I had to help Carl prepare himself for surgery, it had been right to push the knowledge of what lay ahead as far away as possible and to deal with the problem of how to get through the day and then again through the night. But now that was over. There was only one thing I had to deal with now—the possibility of his death.

April 25–May 4, 1972

No, No, one cannot imagine anything in this world, not the least little thing. Everything consists of so many details which cannot be ignored. In the imagination one omits these and does not notice that they are absent, since one moves with such speed. But realities are slow and incredibly detailed.

Rainer Maria Rilke,
The Notebooks of Malte Laurids Brigge

It was the longest day I can remember and that is almost all I can remember about it. I have tried for months to recall the feel and texture of that day, but it is gone. Danny was with me and our dear good friends, Ann and Dolph. I walked the corridors of Eleven East up and down as one walks the floor of a prison cell—endlessly, dully, with the compulsion of the automaton. People kept bringing coffee in plastic containers and hamburgers on paper plates and I looked out of the tall windows in the patients' lounge, where everything is orange-cheerful and painted-bright and where nothing but death sentences and life sentences and disaster sentences are handed out to the frightened relatives who cluster uneasily in the plastic seats around the plastic tables. I remember the overhead light, perpetually bright with the glare of operating room lights; one felt nailed down by it, defenseless, spread-eagled with hands and wrists tied down against the hard surface of the surgery table. No, that was him, not me. But the distinctions blurred.

35

There never was any privacy in that lounge nor anywhere on Eleven East. The huddling relatives would form little tight circles, claiming their table-encompassed territory for their temporary home to shut out the idle curiosity of the clustering group next to them. It was bad form to stare or seem to listen in, yet one did it automatically, expecting perhaps to find some crumb on which to sustain hope for the next half hour. The more fortunate relatives exchanged information on brain tumors and strokes, paralysis and aphasia, blindness, migraine headaches, tottering gait. Everyone's tale had some sort of upbeat ending—he was getting much better; she had the very best doctor on the floor; they were trying a brand-new drug. No one spoke to the relatives of the patient in surgery, just as one does not speak to the prisoner's relatives while the jury is out. Which gave me a lot of time for looking out the window. There was a splendid view of the East River and I hung on to that. As long as the river flows, there is always hope. Waiting in the corridors of the Gestapo headquarters had been like that, a breathless suspense under a blanket of dread. One did not want the waiting to end, for as long as it did not end it might be good. A boat came down the river, then another. Life goes on. As long as there is no messenger, all is well.

Sometime in the afternoon, Dr. Wolbrenner stepped off the elevator. I saw him for a few seconds before he saw me, but I could not call out. He was the messenger. I did not want to hear the message.

Apparently, neither did he want to give it. "All went well so far. They removed a tumor," he said briskly, as though he were about to answer an urgent call elsewhere. "I can't tell you any more about it. Dr. Ambrose will be down shortly. I observed the operation, but I was not assisting, so it will be much better for Dr. Ambrose to speak to you. I'd really rather not answer any questions."

I knew then that it was bad. It was in his eyes before he ever began to speak. His eyes were masked with professionalism. He had to perform an unpleasant duty and he had already begun to guard himself against our anguish. I watched him hurrying down the corridor.

After that I began to mobilize my resources. I remember that part of the day. Walking up and down the corridors and preparing myself for the worst. I knew about that. If you want to survive horror, you have to prepare yourself for the worst. Feel it through, live it through in advance. Then, if it does not happen, you're ahead. If it does, you can bear it. Oh, I knew this as well as I knew anything and I moved into it unconsciously, the way an animal gets ready its defenses for danger.

"Carl and I have had such a good life together," I said to Ann. "If it has to end now—we've been luckier than most. Funny, I was always afraid he'd go first . . ."

"He'll be all right," she said.

Hollow inside, walking the tightrope, tense, dry-mouthed. I tried out the words, but there was no feeling. It was too dangerous to let in feeling.

Dr. Ambrose phoned the nursing station to let me know he'd be down in fifteen minutes. Ten minutes later, a nurse called to say it would take awhile longer. An hour later, he and Dr. Wolbrenner stepped out of the elevator.

"Your husband had a seizure in the recovery room and we had to take him back in. He is fine now," Dr. Ambrose explained the delay. "You can see him in a little while, when they bring him down. Is there anywhere we can talk?"

The young social worker had given me the key to her tiny office, a precious gift of privacy. The two doctors, Danny and I squeezed in. There were only two chairs. I took one, Dr. Ambrose the other. Dr. Wolbrenner sat on the desk. He wore an expensive sport coat and cashmere turtleneck and looked ill at ease. Danny stood behind my chair.

"Do you want your son . . . ?"

"Yes, of course." I was watching Dr. Ambrose's eyes.

They were kind and weary and did not evade me and for an instant I had a flicker of hope.

Dr. Wolbrenner was the first to speak. "It is," he said ceremoniously, "not as bad as the worst of our fears. Nor as good as the best of our hopes." Obviously, this phrase had repeatedly served him on similar occasions.

"Let me have it straight, please," I said. Danny's hands gripped my shoulders.

"Of course," Dr. Ambrose said. The tumor, which had shown on the angiogram, was fairly small and encapsulated and he had, he believed, wholly removed it. But he had also probed somewhat ahead of it and found a larger mass. Because of its location and diffuse shape it was inoperable. He had had to leave it in. "If I had attempted to take it out, I might possibly prolong his life, but there would have been no speech or memory. I thought for Mr. Lerner this would not be a viable solution."

"God, no. Is it malignant?"

"It's an astrocytoma." There were, it appeared, two types of brain tumors. One benign, and various kinds of malignant ones. An astrocytoma was of the latter kind. Dr. Ambrose took a pad out of his white coat pocket and drew something resembling a flower—the center relatively less malignant, the star-shaped offshoots, which might grow in any direction, malignant. "Of course we will not know definitely until the slides are done, but I'm afraid what I saw is unmistakable."

Dr. Wolbrenner launched into a lengthy explanation of the nature of brain tumors. "Malignancy does not have the same meaning in a brain tumor as it does if the tumor is in other parts of the body. Some benign tumors can, because of their location, be as damaging as some malignant ones. Encapsulation does not necessarily—"

"Please, I told you. I want the truth."

"We will give cobalt radiation," Dr. Ambrose said. "That extends the life expectancy. There are also new drugs—"

38

"How much time?"

"Six months, a year. That's statistical evidence. You have to remember, each life is unique. Some people have amazing resources and your husband is such an exceptional person—"

"What are the figures?" Danny asked.

"Five percent survive the first year." Dr. Ambrose looked pained. "But then, statistical evidence is meaningless in the individual case. If a person is among the five percent—"

"You said six months," I interrupted. "What's the percentage on that?"

"Eighty percent don't make it more than six months."

"One thing you should know," Dr. Wolbrenner added, "there is no pain or discomfort with a brain tumor. There can be good and meaningful life right up to the end—"

I was supposed to be pleased at that. "Is his mind—"

"There should be no impairment," Dr. Ambrose said firmly. "His arm and leg are weak—"

"Paralyzed?"

"We should know positively about the leg in a day or so. I'm quite sure it will come back. The arm and hand . . . we just don't know. But we'll start him on rehabilitation right away. Sometimes these people can do amazing things." It went on like this for a while. It was impossible to place all the words together and find a meaning. The hollowness inside me widened; I could feel it vibrate and echo. I was cool and detached; my mind was focused on keeping level on the tightrope. Concentrated on some inner message, keeping steady, one part of me above it all.

Only my mouth was so dry I could barely squeeze the words out. "He may not want cobalt at all. He may not want to live like that—"

"We'll discuss that tomorrow," Dr. Ambrose said gently. "It's too soon now. You've been through quite a day."

"I'm all right."

"You're a very brave woman."

"Dr. Ambrose is right, Mom," Danny said.

Dr. Wolbrenner opened the door. The bright lights of the orange lounge pinned me down to the lab table, spread-eagled, helpless. There were staring faces out there. We walked through them. "Thank you," I said stupidly to Dr. Ambrose. It occurred to me later, what for? For keeping the star-shaped flower in my love's head to flourish and grow and devour him? Meaningful life they call it, and the concept seemed preposterous then, but I did not know. I still did not know. Dr. Ambrose pressed my hand with his limber, knowing surgeon's fingers. Thank you.

Later, they wheeled the stretcher down the hall. He was hooked up to two intravenous tubes. His head was swathed in a white gauze turban which covered his forehead. His eyes were open. We bent over him and he recognized us. He spoke. He was lucid.

My God, he was alive. Still alive.

Then I began to cry.

April 26–27

In the Intensive Care Unit they fight for life with more gadgetry and insistence than imagination can fathom. Monitors are at every bedside, recording the faint thumping of heartbeats, the erratic curves of electric impulse, the aberrations of respiration. Six patients in their separate beds, their separate struggles, linked to the monitoring center, are constantly observed by teams of nurses and doctors. There is no day here, there is no night. A noisy, bustling place, alert at every moment to warning lights, tiny balls jumping up and down on graphs, curves stretching and flattening on overhead screens. Whenever the signals indicate aberrant tracings, when the curves peak or the lines become straight, the white-clad team at the central console table springs into action.

Gadgets, needles, cajoling, shouting. "John, can you

hear me? What's your name? Can you recognize me? John? Move your eyes. Can you feel this? Can you feel?" When they succeed, the curves spring back to life, the thump thump of the monitors joins the general chorus, the still figure on the bed has another chance. Fear, courage, defiance. They literally irritate the patient back to life. They try in the ICU, they certainly try. . . .

In the ICU death hovers on the ceiling, a glittering, sterile, aluminum surface, forever reflecting light and light movements. The doctors consider it a problem, caused by a fault in the architectural design. The glitter of tubing, bedposts and gadgets mingles with the irrepressible reflections of traffic outside the window to produce a dancing light show on the ceiling. The doctors worry because the patients sometimes hallucinate about these lights, seeing them as flickering candles, ghostly death signals. The architects have tried to correct the design with tightly curtained windows, dully painted walls—but nothing seems to help. Mocking the controlling efforts of science, the spectral lights persist in their eerie presence.

Carl is lucky. He is conscious; he can speak. Sometimes it seems they have put him in here by mistake, with all those people. There is a woman in the bed next to him, retching and vomiting almost continuously. We draw the curtain between the beds; we turn our eyes elsewhere. But where?

The man in the bed opposite is in his forties. His wife and two daughters are at his bedside constantly. A handsome man; they have removed a brain tumor, but he seizured after the surgery and lost his speech. His body recovering, he lies mute. The wife and daughters talk to him as one talks to a deaf man; they read the paper to him. He grunts, chokes, waves his hands. The nurses say he will learn to speak by hand signals. Some of them speak by blinking their eyelids, yes and no, mostly.

Carl seizured after surgery, but he is wide awake and alert. None of his faculties are affected. A paralyzed arm, a weak leg, that seems like nothing here. Carl is lucky.

By the door lies a very old man. He is totally paralyzed, lying like a corpse all the days and nights. His
lips are parted by a clamp; from each nostril hangs a
tube connected to a bottle with liquid. His eyelids are
taped open, the arms and hands tied down on a board.
Tubes for intravenous feeding are attached to his arms
and legs; catheter tubes emerge from the lower part of the
body. He is hooked up to an EKG machine; his pressure
and other vital data appear on TV monitors. His body,
through the machines, sends out signals and he is marvelously cared for by many hands—washed, turned,
shifted, cranked upright, his kidneys flushed, his bowels
emptied. Sometimes a young girl, perhaps sixteen years
old, poorly dressed and looking neglected, sits at the foot
of the old man's bed. She stares at him, once or twice
calls his name and touches his hand. Then she leaves,
her shoulders hunched forward. He never responds to
anything. "Deep coma," the nurses call it. They will not
say how long he's been like that. Some of the nurses believe firmly that people can feel and think even in deep
coma, although doctors don't admit it. Each time I
come into the room or leave it, I have to pass that old
man. I make my eyes sweep over him unseeing, but I
take it all in, anyway. I put my chair so Carl cannot see
him, but it's probably useless.

April 29

Carl is lucky. He has the bed by the window,
and during the time when it's day outside, they let us
open the curtains. He can see the traffic rolling by. He
likes seeing the river; it connects him with life.
There is a terrible room at the end of the corridor,
where they keep a young woman. I've seen her, she is
quite pretty. She got her brain tumor during pregnancy
and they delivered the baby by cesarean before they did
the surgery for the tumor. The baby is fine, I'm told, a
girl, and the mother's tumor was removed, so there is
hope she will recover, only she has become blind. She

shrieks, whenever the drugs wear off, day and night. She keeps shouting about not being able to see her baby. Her husband and parents huddle in the lounge; they talk about how it will all be better once they get her home. I try not to pass that room.

The rules in the ICU are that they let you in for twenty minutes once every hour. So you are sort of privileged, compared to the regular visitors. You are permitted to spend your day in the hospital, no particular visiting hours, just that rule. And another—whenever they do anything for any of the other patients, all visitors must leave. They are very sticky about that rule in the ICU, but we relatives get to know everything anyway. We become part of the hospital's pulse and rhythm.

Yesterday, the young girl who visits the old man sat outside on the bench, crying. I spoke to her and she told me she is the old man's granddaughter; there is no other family. The nurses had told her he might be dying that day, but she'd waited all day and now it was the same thing as always. She was afraid to stay and afraid to leave. I brought her some coffee and went and told the social worker about her and the social worker talked to her and after a while she left. The old man died during the night. The nurses pulled all the curtains around each bed and sent the visitors to the far end of the hall. Doors were closed and the service elevator was called up and everything was done so quietly and efficiently it caused less commotion than when they wheel a post-surgery case through the halls. When the curtains were opened, all the gadgets had been removed and the mattress was off the bed and it took a little while before they sterilized everything and put clean new sheets on the bed, ready for the next patient. "He's gone, he died," was the first thing Carl said when I came back into the room. He notices everything. Has the old man's death the same meaning for him as for me—the ultimate horror, mechanical death? I have tried talking to the doctors about it; they grow evasive at once when the word "coma" is mentioned. Dr. Ambrose said it might be a kind form of

43

death, "the brain protecting itself from knowledge." Nobody says so, but it is obviously considered bad form for me to have noticed the old man at all.

Waiting outside once more, sitting on an unused stretcher for the sake of variety, I try to think of what a good death might be. The only death to which I have come even faintly close was that of Carl's father. Pop, a very sweet, simple man, died neatly and quietly, as he had lived. He sat in a chair, sweat-covered with the effort of breathing and watched the snow falling outside. He talked to me of the few fundamentals, of Mom, of our children (his only grandchildren), of Carl, Reba (the worry over her not working), Charlie (the perpetual worry over Charlie's eyes). Then about his second marriage—all at once the false things fell off; he dismissed it. He was unhappy in the life of his old age; he would be intolerably unhappy, offended in his dignity and self-respect, if he continued as an invalid. He did not want that kind of life for his last years. It would have been different, if Mom were with him now. . . . He loved to sit by the window and watch the falling snow, he said, and smiled on his death-kissed face.

I tried to encourage him about going to the hospital, speaking about the need for keeping his spirits up, helping the doctors and so on. He looked at me patiently, as though he had neither heard nor understood. Suddenly, his blue eyes seemed to twinkle; his hand waved me off. "Sure," he said, "fight the case, that's what you mean." He nodded, the face froze again. Fight the case. He promised that.

In the hospital, his skin grew lighter and very fine to the touch. There was a sort of concentrated, essential quality to his face, as though death had stripped all the unimportant qualities off and only the core remained. That sparkle of life in the blue eyes, the deep twinkle of humor which enabled him to joke on our last visit and make the nurses laugh. A good man, who had lived a simple, good life. He summed it up for himself: "I have good children." He made the parting easy, because he

44

had that kind of courage. "Go away," he said, "what do you want to hang around here for—" waving away the son and daughter-in-law he loved.

I remember looking back at him as we left: emaciated body, feverish skin, pumped up, literally, with borrowed life, unable to make his own blood, living on enormous transfusions, he sat up in bed and laughed. Insisted on sitting and looked out of his shrunken face with bright and cunning eyes. Perhaps I'll die, he seemed to say, I'll die most likely. But not just yet, not this minute. Still fighting the case.

He talked to the doctors a half hour before he died and said he felt fine. There was no part of his body the cancer had not eaten. But to the very end it did not touch his soul.

Yes, I thought, Pop's death was a good death. Maybe Carl will have his luck, I said to myself. Stop looking at the nightmares here. He will have such luck. I noticed that once again my hand was playing with the pin I had been wearing for five days, for good luck. The silver pin of two birds touching, which Carl had given me as his first gift.

The door was open for visitors, and I went back into the ICU.

May 1972

To see and to know
is to suffer twice

before it begins
cobweb castle of
mind construction

choking on threads
of my own making
struggling on the hook

there is no answer
for the fish
as there is

                        no answer, Lord
                        no answer
for me

Our separation began the day after surgery. We battled on separate battlefields, each very much alone. Mine: to prepare myself for his death, to help him to die a good death. His: to live.

Bald-headed, his arm still hooked to the intravenous, half of his body paralyzed, he lay in the ICU under the flickering lights, exposed to the incessant bustle of nurses and technicians and to the sounds of four other patients struggling with various crises of their systems. He was alert, regained his brilliant smile, his indomitable vitality. He would make it, it didn't matter how. He began physical therapy the day after surgery. He

49

grinned at passing nurses, hooked residents and attendants with his charm and good spirits, commanded visitors to his bedside and radiated confidence and strength. He would make it—they all believed it, even those who knew better. Those who knew better believed he would make it for longer than anyone before him; the others allowed themselves the illusion of faith. From the start Carl banished depression and gloom from his periphery, projecting this attitude so strongly all those who came in contact with him absorbed it. It was the actor in him—he understood the potency of assuming a role and projecting it to others. Thus, barely released from the ICU, free from the intravenous and allowed to create his environment within the confines of his corner room, he became himself again.

He followed all sensible orders, but insisted on respectful and individualized treatment by everyone. He involved himself in every detail. His usual perfectionism, which had made him the awe and dread of his students and professional colleagues, asserted itself at once. He used his considerable charm to hold those around him to a meticulous performance of every service he needed. Everything had to be done just right.

He threw himself enthusiastically into the rehabilitation exercises and worked on them without giving in to fatigue. The Rehab people adored him; he had just the spirit they tried to arouse in the despairing, gloomy wrecks with whom they daily worked. The results of his efforts, which began to show up in a few weeks, were most gratifying. Inch by inch, his leg was coming back to life. Within six weeks, he was able to walk, with a weak and tottering gait, but walk. He pursued the rehabilitation of his arm with equally dogged persistence. He practiced endlessly, accepted passive exercise, massage and every kind of therapy, never losing faith that the dead, sluggish limb would gradually come back, as the leg was coming back. He never succumbed to the boredom and hopelessness of it all. Nothing ever diminished his superb self-assurance and dignity. He did it all his own way, which is perhaps all anyone can hope for at the end.

Cobalt radiation was started about two weeks after surgery. He received massive doses, the maximum number of treatments allowable. He was warned of the side effects: drowsiness, nausea, extreme fatigue, loss of hair. But none of it happened, except loss of hair on the radiated side. He never questioned why radiation was being given; he simply went daily, did his exercises, ate his meals and created, on this tough and wise ward, a unique position for himself.

Perhaps it started with his refusal to wear hospital clothes. As soon as he could sit up he insisted on his own clothing, his daily shave, his habitual, meticulous grooming. A few weeks after surgery, when he was first being taken down to the Rehab Institute for his daily exercises, he requested that I bring him a certain set of pants and shirt. That morning, he appeared in the Rehab group session among all the handicapped patients in their shapeless, striped hospital bathrobes, attired in pinstripe slacks, a red belt, red shirt and blue blazer. I was not present, but I understand he caused a sensation as he was being wheeled down the corridors. The next day, one other man wore a shirt and pants. The third day several more. By the end of the week, the entire group in Rehab appeared in their own clothes and—as the physiotherapist later told me—with very much higher morale.

He remembered the faces and names of each person who attended him, whether nurse or orderly or clerk. His room was always full of flowers, cards and visitors. He talked about walking when he could not move the leg, about writing when his arm hung limp by his side, about going home when he was barely able to sit and about going back to work, as soon as he was out in the wheelchair. He was adored by his nurses; he managed to establish a unique and personal relationship with each of his doctors. An ideal patient.

He refused to look me in the face. He sent me away

when I tried to speak to him, he rejected my efforts at nursing him, preferring the available professional services, and treated me, so it seemed to me then, not much more personally than the private duty nurse he had just acquired. I was baffled, angered, hurt by it all. I stormed out of the room, sitting dazed in the corridor, crying if anyone spoke to me at all. He was rejecting me and I did not understand why.

One night a kind black male nurse found me out in the hall, crying. He asked me what the trouble was. I told him. "I've seen it many times," he reassured me. "The men that don't care much for their wives treat them okay. But a man who loves his wife, when he's down like that—handicapped—seems like he treats his wife like dirt. Seems like he can't stand the idea of what it's doing to you."

He comforted me and we went on talking for quite a while. This was the beginning of my education by nurses, orderlies and attendants. They had learned from experience and were willing to share with me. I had much to learn.

The very morning after surgery the Irish day supervisor took me into her office and told me bluntly that I must tell him the truth about his condition. "Don't listen to the doctors, don't listen to your family. They'll all cop out on you. I've seen it happen a hundred times. You've got to tell him the truth because he'll find out sooner or later and it just makes it so much harder for all of you." I quite agreed with her; she was saying just what I believed. Only, as she went on telling me case histories and offering encouragement, I got sicker and sicker. She made me promise to read Dr. Kubler-Ross's book, *On Death and Dying*, and sent me out to get used to the routine of the relatives of intensive care patients.

I ran into problems with the doctors at once. The day after surgery I consulted with Dr. Ambrose and Dr. Wolbrenner and asked their advice again about whether to tell Carl the truth. They both advised strongly against it. They had different viewpoints, but agreed that it was dangerous and destructive to tell a patient he was terminal. Dr. Wolbrenner assured me that patients never wanted to know the truth, no matter what they said before the illness. It seemed to him to be almost a psychological law, an inner need. You could tell them and they would not hear it; they would refuse to accept it. He pointed out to me that Carl had not asked whether the tumor was malignant.

"Well, it's only the second day."

"Precisely. Why don't you just wait and see if he asks? I predict he won't. Most patients don't."

I was not satisfied with that statement. "I know this man," I insisted. "I've lived with him for thirty-two years and we have never lied to each other. I can't lie to him now, I won't. I must tell him the truth."

Dr. Ambrose's reasoning was different. He told a—to me—very touching anecdote. As a young intern before World War II he had frequently seen patients die of pneumonia. Pneumonia was an incurable disease. Then, antibiotics were discovered and, within one week, no more deaths. Since that time he felt he could never say to a patient or to his family, you will die within a certain time. One never knew what might happen—

"Miracles?"

"Why not?" said Dr. Ambrose. I looked at his gentle, wise face, his beautiful hands which were courageous enough to enter other men's brains with knives, and envied him his faith. I really trusted this man, but I knew I could not follow his advice. All I could do, out of respect for him and his judgment, was to wait until Carl asked, or at least until the end of radiation.

The next day an old friend, himself a surgeon, whom I trusted and admired greatly, came to visit Carl at the ICU. Afterward, he asked me to come downstairs for a cup of coffee. We took paper containers out into the fresh air, then sat for about twenty minutes in his car and talked. He came right to the point. Did Carl know? Did I intend to tell him?

"No, he does not know. And yes, I do intend to tell him."

Almost in the same words, he gave me Dr. Ambrose's argument. And on top of it, Dr. Wolbrenner's. He himself had seen it happen so many times before: patients needed hope. To the last moment of life a patient needs hope. Take hope away and you kill a person more surely than the cancer kills him.

This man has been our doctor and our friend for twenty years. He is a rare human being, courageous and humanist. I could not disregard his judgment, nor take his words lightly. But I could not accept them, either. "First of all, I don't see how I can carry it off even if I wanted to—"

"You're strong, you can do it." These words which I would hear frequently in the coming months seemed less than a compliment to me. If I were strong, I would do what I thought was right. If not, I wasn't strong.

"That's really not the point. What's at issue is his right to make decisions about himself. He may not want to go through with radiation, with any of the other treatments, if he knows—"

"Carl has enormous vitality. Besides, almost every patient I've ever seen wants to live, no matter what. It's human nature."

"That's what you have to say, as a doctor. I don't have to say that; I already know he has a cancer eating away at his brain and before long he may not be able to make sensible decisions. I've got to tell him the truth, while he still can think and act for himself. Don't you understand that?"

We then discussed the crux of the matter. Was I prepared for the fact he might want to kill himself if he knew? Did I think he would? And if I thought so, would I still tell him?

I did not know what he would do when told the truth. But even if I knew, I would still have to tell him.

Our friend pointed out that most likely all I would accomplish was to make the last months of his life painful, agonizing and full of inner conflict. If I just let him believe he still had a chance, it would be easier on him.

There was no answer to such an argument. Nor was there an answer to his impassioned plea for me simply to wait. It felt like yet another stone added to the weight I was carrying. All I knew was that I could not put it down. The more everyone told me to do what I believed to be wrong, the heavier the load became.

My problem was made more difficult because it also involved a decision I had to make about Stephanie. Our daughter, who was still in Europe, had been told about Carl's illness and the surgery, but she did not yet know that there was no hope for recovery. I had wanted to tell her the truth from the beginning, but Dr. Ambrose had flatly interdicted any emergency visit before the surgery and had strongly advised against it immediately afterward. There was no question in my mind that Stephanie would insist on coming home, if she knew. Dr. Ambrose had explained at length that any kind of excitement, pleasant or otherwise, can have the most disastrous consequences after brain surgery. Carl had seizured in the operating room, which meant that there was considerable danger of seizures during the first postsurgery weeks. There was reason to believe that her arrival would produce some tension in Carl, for there had been some conflict between Stephanie and us due to her refusal to leave India right after her accident. Under normal circumstances we could have talked it out and settled it face to face, but a man in Carl's condition was not likely to be able to handle conflicting emotions without excitement and stress. For these reasons all the doctors urged, with great unanimity, that Stephanie not come to see him until after radiation therapy was over. Another part of their reasoning was that having her come so suddenly from abroad would make Carl suspect that his illness was terminal. If he actually took a turn for the worse, she could always come within a few

A Death of One's Own

hours. One lie leads to another, I thought bitterly, feeling entrapped by this double argument yet unable to take the responsibility for the medical consequences.

For a few days I consulted and canvassed many opinions. Every doctor to whom I spoke agreed with Dr. Ambrose. I must not tell Carl the truth—he did not want to hear it and I would only add to his burdens. They made me feel that all I was trying to do was relieve my own feelings. If I would truly consider him, I would say nothing and encourage him to have hope. The only one to disagree was our friend, the psychoanalyst. He thought I should tell him and I most likely would, but advised me to tell him when he seemed to want to know.

I took that advice and rejected the others. In rejecting it, which was much harder than can be conveyed in the retelling, an enormous load of anger and bitterness began to build up inside of me. I felt I had to stand up to all the knowing experts. I had to stand alone, or almost alone, and take all the responsibility upon myself. It took me a few weeks to understand that that was exactly what was required of me. I would have to take the full responsibility for everything from here on out. That was the only way in which I could help Carl. So that was what I would do.

Slowly, I began the process of disciplining my feelings. I would have to learn to take whatever Carl imposed, without, as had been my habit in three decades of marriage, standing my ground and making my own needs known. This was all past. Now only his needs counted and I would have to learn to subordinate myself to them. The beginning was hard, but then it became quite easy. It even gave me a sort of satisfaction, simply as an act of love.

One thing for sure—he did not want to know. I began to interpret his aloofness, his deliberate keeping me at a distance, as his way of letting me know that he did not want to know. He had asked me, the day after surgery, "Was it malignant?" to which I had truthfully replied,

"We won't know till the biopsy comes in—that'll be in about a week." Then he never asked me again. That was a clue.

Further—cobalt radiation. Carl was a highly educated, well-informed man. He knew very well that cobalt radiation is never used except in the case of malignancy. Yet he never questioned me or the doctors why he was being given radiation. I took this as another clue. He did not want to know. Not then.

In retrospect I am sorry I did not follow my instinct, my inclination and my convictions. I should have told him then and there. If he did not want to believe it, as probably he did not, he would have found a way to disregard it. But he would have known his trust in me could remain unbroken and it would have saved me months of agony and emotional separation from him. I'm certain now that his efforts at distancing himself from me were based on his full emotional knowledge that I was the messenger with the deadly news. As long as he could keep me at a distance, he need not know. Had he known right away, he would have had the comfort of our being together emotionally, as we would later be.

It was bad advice I got and I believe it stemmed, unconsciously and though offered with the best of intentions, from a profound fear and denial of death. It is most difficult for human beings to accept the randomness and unfairness of death. Death is implacable, out of reach of human control. This is the essence of the human condition and humankind has tried forever to wriggle out of it. Science tries to foil death by postponing it and controlling disease. Each cure perfected becomes "proof" of the success of science in its battle with death. Yet it only means that death inhabits the living for longer. As we conquer more of the formerly fatal ailments, we increase the number of the aged living in the shadow of death without increasing their ability to deal philosophically and emotionally with the inevitable end. Our culture makes it very difficult for the individual to accept the fact of death and to die with dignity. The isolation of the dying from the living, our denial and ignorance of their needs and their plight, corrode our living existence, harass us with fears and weight us down with guilt. But death must be faced; it must be met. Dying is part of the experience of living. I had to struggle six bitter months by myself and Carl had to struggle by himself until we could come together and face what we needed to face. The experts are wrong. By denying the patient the truth we don't make his end easier. We just cushion the shock to ourselves. The dying must be accepted into the community of the living until they are actually dead; we must stop their cruel and unnecessary isolation. The terminal patient has no time for subterfuge and denial. If he does not want to hear the truth, he will shut it out. But if he does want to hear it, who are we to keep it from him? It is his death, not ours. Every man and woman has the right to his or her own death.

During those early weeks I was restless and miserable whenever I was away from Carl. The only place where I felt calm was in his room. Even when he slept, as he did for long daylight hours, I would sit quietly in a corner, reading or dozing, and feel that everything was all right. It was not altruism that made me stay, it was a form of self-preservation, even greed. I wanted to share his experience, the sights he could see, the sounds surrounding him. I wanted to watch, observe, participate.

Being there made it possible for me to keep in touch with nurses, doctors and all the minute daily decisions which could make his life more comfortable. I could get his meals from the outside. Once I kept him from being given an unnecessary test, which had been written on his chart and later canceled. I wrote letters for him, read to him, regulated the flow of visitors. In truth, I was there because I wanted every minute I could get with him. And because I was afraid of being outside, alone. Superstitiously afraid.

They allowed me to stay in the hospital as late as I wanted. Until Carl fell asleep. He would not fall asleep until we had followed a meticulous, neurotic routine which began at ten and ended after eleven thirty. The orderlies gave him his night care—straightened the sheets, back rub, face wash. Then the room had to be fixed just so, the curtains drawn a certain way, the table aligned properly at the foot of the bed, the flowers moved behind the double window curtains. He was afraid, I think, as one always is in hospital rooms when the darkness creeps in and opens hidden passages into the soul. The sounds of stillness fill the breath and expand perception from within. Everything vibrates and rustles. One listens to one's heartbeat, a noisy pump, and the hollow spaces of night open. Nothing to impede it. Death enters stealthily, crouches at the foot of the bed, snickers. The breath becomes choking. One is alone.

He was afraid and would not admit it. He would not hold my hand or speak or cry. When I kissed him good night, he controlled it, play-acted. It was terrifying to him to show—or even allow himself to feel—his true feelings. And yet, over the years, we had developed the kind of relationship in which he felt as free to express himself as I did. Now, his bravery was an iron shirt which held him upright and kept me from getting near him. But he dreaded the night and contrived all that childish procedure to keep me in the room.

I hated this routine. It was wearisome, tedious and futile. The pills would finally put him to sleep anyway, and the time spent in this sham dance only kept us more apart. I felt like slipping into bed beside him to hug him tightly—later, at home, I would sometimes do it. I wanted to rock him, to sing German lullabies to him, which sometimes had helped to put him to sleep. Instead, I did empty, repetitious motions, placing the flashlight an inch to the right, the bell slightly closer to the head of the bed and so on. He checked my every gesture. It reminded me of the way my grandmother had supervised the maid, a memory which humiliated me. I understood very well that a helpless man, out of control of everything that matters, must have something to control, even if it is only the position of the night table. I understood that a man without a right arm and unable to move his right leg must borrow my arms and legs to tyrannize the environment into granting him power. He was seeking for magic and it was not me he meant to control. I was simply his tool, and in a way, to let myself be used that way and know he could accept it from me was a form of expressing friendship. I understood all that, but after a long day it was hard to take.

Another thing it did was to alter our relationship in a way I did not want to accept. He was infantilizing himself, acting like a spoiled child, putting me into the position of mother. He demanded and exerted the tyranny of the helpless. In so doing, he made me share his helplessness, truly experience it. I raged inside, as he must have raged inside, and with his usual acuteness for my moods, he knew it. It is strange to believe, but we quarreled for some weeks, silently, stubbornly struggling against each other. What it really was about was acceptance or denial of his condition.

I remember walking out of the room near midnight into the quiet, half-dark corridors, carrying my shopping bags full of his dirty laundry and my resentment, aching with fatigue. The night shift nurses nodded sympathetically. It felt nice to think of their approval for my steadiness and persistence. Not so nice to drive home at excessive speed, letting out the rage and impatience in carelessness, then coming home to the empty apartment.

Inevitably, during those weeks, Rumpel, our high-strung Siamese cat, had shown his distress over my neglect of him by vomiting all over the living room rug. I cleaned it up, gagging, fed both cats, petted Rumpel to settle him down. Then, it really began for me.

I would fix myself a drink and sit in the living room,

Rumpel contentedly purring beside me, giving some life to the empty spaces on the sofa. I tried to relax, to forget. But my mind worked like a steam drill. All the thoughts I had pushed aside all day came out sharp as knives: the young woman in the corner room, screaming over her blindness; the staggering old man, half out of his mind in the ward room; the man in the ICU who had lost his speech. I saw them before me—they were the next stages. It might be one, it might be another, it might be all of them. It would get so that night routine, which seemed so unbearable now, would be something easy and gentle to look back upon. From the horror images my mind switched back to the myriad of unsolved daily problems: how to find nurses if I wanted to keep him home; how to go on working if I did. If I gave up working, how long would I be able to stand it in that room incessantly, as things became worse? . . . The children—when would their nerve give out? Money. The insurance would surely run out in a few months. From how much of this should I protect him? From how much of it could I? He would want to be dead much sooner than he could be dead. What if he could not ask me the questions he wanted to ask? What if he could no longer tell me what he wanted done? What if his mind went?

Friends sometimes asked me if I was not afraid, staying alone in the apartment all night, if I was not terribly lonely. I was never afraid in the sense in which they meant the question. What I had to deal with was so much more terrifying than anything that could happen to me, being alone almost felt comforting. I needed that time each night, to sort out my feelings, to allow the nightmares to come up and become familiar. Later, when there would never be an hour of being alone anywhere, I longed for the quiet, free misery of those earlier nights.

It was usually too late to call anyone and there was no one, really, I wanted to call. As it was I felt terribly indebted to my good friends on whom I placed, quite shamelessly, the inordinate burden of making themselves available to me whenever I needed them. There comes a point when there is very little left for even the best friends to say or do.

Despite the warm summer nights, I was always freezing. It was impractical to take a sleeping tablet, since I had to be up at 7:30 for the call from the night nurse. I picked up a book, any book, and read until the letters swam before my eyes. Took another drink till I felt rocky. Sometimes—perhaps those were the lucky nights—I threw myself on the floor and cried, often sobbing loudly, hoping that, by some miracle, someone would hear and come and tell me it was all a nightmare and everything would go away. After a while, crying like this would calm me and I would finally go to sleep. I slept lightly those nights, always waiting for the phone call.

I lived close to the edge of exhaustion during those early weeks. Increasingly fretful and impatient during the night routine, I realized this could not go on and that I might be heading for a breakdown. But worse, something between Carl and me was being destroyed before it needed to be destroyed. It took me quite a while before I could come to a decision. I realized, thinking about it in those long hours before going to sleep, that what was at stake was the way we were going to handle the rest of the time we had. Hiding our fear, evading it neurotically, each bearing our pain alone—that way lay self-destruction. That way we were losing more than we needed to lose.

Still, I did not quite know how to do it. I tried to explain to Carl how difficult it was for me to stay so late at the hospital each day. I encouraged him to tell me how he felt when I left, how the nights were for him.

He would not; he turned his face aside. That night, angrily, he sent me away at 9:30. "Go on home, I can manage without you." I went, weeping in the hall and all the way home. The night nurse told me he was up half the night and needed an extra sleeping tablet. Dr. Ambrose, with whom I discussed the problem, gave orders for Carl's medication to be given earlier and spoke to him about the need to have lights out by ten. But he was as reluctant as I was to risk upsetting Carl. It would serve no purpose to change his routine, if it would make him tense and give him sleepless nights. Also, there was always the danger of tension creating seizures.

I consulted some of the nurses and orderlies. Someone, I have forgotten whom, said Carl was pushing me to see how far I would go, because handicapped men got that way with the people closest to them. And that probably the worst thing for Carl was to see me giving in that way. He knew me and knew this was a sign of how bad I thought things were. Whoever said this helped me to focus on the real problem.

He was helpless; he was crippled. But there were many things he could still do for himself. I was allowing him to become more helpless than he needed to be. I was also doing something quite abnormal in our relationship: I was suppressing my angry feelings. When he was wrong, I pretended it was all right. Obviously, he knew this and read it as an alarming sign of my fear for him. It seemed as if I was beginning to act from guilt.

I thought about that, long and hard. Once guilt enters this kind of situation, it's a roller coaster downhill. This had to stop. I would have to accept the fact that there were limits to what I could do for him: I would have to do everything I could and no more.

That evening I told him that I was leaving at ten because I needed to get more rest. Pure egotism, but there it was. I thought he could manage things in such a way that we could get through easily before then and we even could have time to sit quietly together before I had to leave. He said nothing and dragged his routine out, as usual. I told him it was five minutes to ten. He told me to leave anytime I wanted. I said, You're not as helpless as you think. You can help yourself at night. Everything is within easy reach. I showed him, but he refused to look and sent me away. This time I let him see I was upset by his behavior. It was difficult to leave him like this.

Once on the way home, I was full of guilt. I was terrified he might have a seizure, but the night was uneventful. The next day he sulked and I teased him, which was the way we usually worked out of little quarrels. "I see you're acting like yourself again," I said.

That night, though he was anxious, he was very cooperative. When I kissed him good night, a few minutes after ten, he held me for a moment and really kissed me. "Get some rest, honey," he said. I felt elated. He had accepted his old role again. From then on we managed by ten or perhaps ten thirty.

It remained unspoken, but it was quite clear that something important had been settled during this brief episode. Whatever the limitations imposed upon us, we would, from here on out, live as we always had. If there were differences between us, we would have it out the best we could. We might even quarrel, but we wouldn't live in a damn cocoon. I would not cripple him any more than he was already crippled. As long as he, of his own free will, could do something for me, even just by giving me some time for myself, he was still himself, the man he had always been.

I encountered the devil late one night in the right-hand corridor of Eleven East. He was tall, stooped, distinguished-looking in a sloppy way, with a certain look of seediness about him. His sparse hair was longer than one might have expected in a man his age and was combed back behind his ears. He had cavernous eyes, a large, sad nose and expressive hands. He came out of a private room, carrying something in a paper bag, and hurried down the corridor toward the patients' lounge. I had seen him walk like this before, with a loping gait and a harried, indrawn expression. He never paid any attention to anyone and always seemed preoccupied. That night, as we walked past each other in the corridor, he gave me a penetrating look which, for some reason, made me shiver.

A short while later, on my way to the elevator, I

noticed him sitting in the hideous brightness of the orange-yellow lounge. He sat hunched forward in one of the plastic chairs, fitting it poorly since he was much too tall for it. He was drinking something from what appeared to be a mason jar stuck in the brown paper bag. I found the sight oddly embarrassing.

"Wait a minute," he called out. "Let me talk to you." His mouth was soft and sensuous. He spoke with a Latin accent, perhaps Mexican. His voice sounded sad and anxious, the way the voices of the relatives at Eleven East so often sounded. One did not ignore that tone. I turned toward him and found him half-rising. "Will you sit down a minute?"

I did. "Just a minute, though." Ahead of me was the overly fast ride home, the empty apartment, the long lonely night.

"I noticed you," he said. "You're here even later than I am. Who—"

"My husband. He had brain surgery." We identify ourselves here by our diseases. Obviously he wanted to talk about "his" sickness, but found it hard to get started.

"Ah." His long fingers, bunched over the brown paper bag, were trembling. His shirt was wrinkled, slightly dirty. He obviously was not even going to go through the motions of faking interest in "my" case. "Can I offer you a drink?" he asked absently. "I always have something with me. Don't get bothered by the looks of it. It's Chivas Regal."

I declined. "Who are you here with?"

"My wife. We live in this place. Two years and two months. She's terminal. Metastasized brain cancer. All over her body. Constant pain."

"I'm very sorry." I got up and rang for the elevator. The last thing I wanted to hear was someone else's horror story. Besides which the man made me uneasy.

"I have to go myself," he explained, as he stood next to me baring his bad teeth in what appeared to be an attempt at a grin. "I'm taking her home tomorrow. Have to get back here early."

"Well, at least you can take her home," I said with false cheerfulness, just to fill the time. The elevator came and he stepped in beside me. I would have trouble getting rid of him, I could see.

"I'm taking her to my place out in East Hampton. Two private nurses. Taking her out there to die. She's been dying for two years, nothing the doctors can do. In and out of the hospital, I lost count how many times. Now they don't want her anymore. Did you know they don't let you die in this place?" He grinned his ugly grin and grabbed my elbow. I wrenched free. "The day they finally give up trying their damn experiments, they tell you take her home, we can't do a thing for her. I said, why not keep her here where she's got good care? This is not a nursing home, they tell me. Damn them, for two years we been in and out of here—"

"Yes. Well, good night—" We had stepped out of the elevator into the closed-off section near the front entrance. After 10:00 P.M., in order to exit, one had to walk down several long corridors into the next building. He knew this as well as I did and followed close by my side.

"How's your husband doing?" With apparent effort he managed that obligatory introductory conversation opener in Neurosurgery. It was just common politeness to listen to another person's troubles for at least as long as you expected to be listened to for your troubles.

"Very well," I said determinedly, "he's responding beautifully to chemotherapy."

"Yeah, so did my wife. I remember that stage. Two, three months of euphoria. They tried every goddam new drug on her—she weighs eighty-six pounds now. Can hardly see her, nothing but bones."

"Every case is different," I mumbled. "You have to remember that."

His step kept up with mine in the long dark corridor between the buildings. I was not afraid of him in the ordinary sense, although I was convinced by then he was either quite drunk or somewhat crazy. He posed no threat to me, but I was terrified. It seemed to me he was following me down the corridor, trying to hook his long fingers into me, trying to hang his misery and his sickness on me. "Are you sure you don't want to have a drink with me?" he insisted. "Just one drink so we can talk."

"I'm quite tired." It took considerable effort to put a distant courtesy into my voice. Manners, I thought, good upbringing, to keep the jungle away.

He kept on talking in a low, insinuating monotone, obviously talking to himself. I could hear him thus in the subway, on the way home, perhaps in the emptiness of the room where he hid out between hospital visits. He spoke ugly, intimate details about his wife's illness. He said he did not think she'd live a week out there in East Hampton. He swore to bring her back in an ambulance, so they would have to take her. He cursed the doctors. "You look at me now," he said, "and you trying to get away. I don't blame you." His fingers shook.

I looked at our feet on the beautifully polished floor. His shoes were dusty, ill-kept, very expensive.

"Just wait," he said.

I heard *that*. The devil, I thought. He's after me, the way that hearse was after me on the parkway. Couldn't shake it for the eighteen miles it took to drive to work. Now it's the devil, trying to put his hook into me and drag me down there with him. I swung to face him, feeling angry enough to hit him.

There were tears in his dark eyes; his stringy neck looked old and ugly like the neck of a turkey. "I'm sorry." It seemed he could read my anger. "I've no right— Listen, anytime you want a drink, just come down to the room; I always keep something handy."

"You're going home tomorrow," I said stupidly.

"We'll be back," he said and walked away into the dark parking lot.

I sat in my car for five minutes trying to stop shaking. That's what I would be like in six months, a year. That was the future.

May–June 1972

PARALYSIS

It looks like a hand: warm and supple,
capable of infinite possibilities.   Reach;
grasp; lifting weight; tending tool.

Fingers grown clumsy shape air
instead of surface.   Plastic claw
grasps invisible marbles.   Still,

it feels, sending messages through
choking pathways.   Faulty measurement;
range distorted.   Stiffening joints block

crusted signals.   Wrist and elbow, marvels,
silently rust.   Something twitches—
flutter of the death-tipped bird.

Reach, grasp, touch out of reach—
sagging muscle flapping canvass
over empty tent.   It is still
supple.   It looks like a hand.

Carl was in the hospital for thirteen weeks after surgery. The period, which while I lived through it I perceived as one of acute horror, was actually a salutary time of transition and preparation. The hospital environment, with its trained staff and incredibly rich facilities, provided a cushion to experience. It offered accepted roles, a predetermined routine, constant stimuli and often irritation, which was therapeutic, a sort of diversion. If I could be kept occupied by fighting the accounting department's bureaucracy, one of the few arenas where it still seemed possible for me to win minor victories, it was easier to get through the next twenty-four hours. I had settled in my mind some time ago that the way I would pull this was twenty-four hours at a time—no looking backward, no looking forward. That's as good a formula as I know for extreme situations and it's never yet failed to work. The hospital, a huge, anonymous organism, quickly absorbed us in its rhythms, and turned us into minor actors on its crowded stage. One forgot very quickly that there was a normal world out there and became a part of that *Magic Mountain* world which existed within the air-conditioned, sound-controlled walls against a backdrop of the East River Drive and the constant bridge traffic. Activity rarely ceased within that private room. Outside, in the corridors, nursing quarters and lounges, a familiar cast of characters was in cyclic motion. We became so much a part of it that a new patient or the departure of an old one, the vacation of an orderly or the weekend absence of certain nurses, were "events" in our lives.

The theatricality of it all was enhanced by Carl's dramatic change of appearance: his emergence first from the white cloth turban, the quick regrowth of hair, the brief period of normalcy, then the quick balding on the irradiated side, the change in his features from drug reaction, the change in his posture from paralysis. We furnished the stage with all the old props we could muster: paintings and photos from home, his familiar brash and stylish clothing, a greenhouse display of plants and flowers, trusted and friendly books. I was constantly occupied with the scheduling of a never-ending flow of visitors, the answering of phone calls, the providing of meals. His appetite, always rebellious toward the hospital food, declined once radiation started and he would eat no hospital meal except breakfast. I brought in all his meals and friends provided lavish treats, such as a corn-beef-on-rye catered feast from Reubens and hot mandarin dishes brought in napkin-covered containers. I juggled schedules endlessly in order to wait for his doctors, for the quick—always disturbing—conferences in corridors or unused treatment rooms. It was a harassing and busy time. Later I would think back on it as a relatively easy time when everything was laid out for me and there were many hands to do what was needed, many heads to make decisions, many people willing to take responsibility.

Like all people in institutions we kept ourselves occupied by laying vain plans for escape and plotting against the authorities. We delighted in breaking or circumventing minor regulations. Routine complaints became settings for venting our frustration and helplessness. For me, in particular, these minor battles became inflated in significance. Like Carl, I was entrapped by helplessness, which I found impossible to accept. This was a sensation I remembered very well from the period of Nazi occupation. For five months, after they released me and my mother from jail, we lived under an order of deportation. We were supposed to leave the country within two weeks on pain of being sent to a concentration camp. The trouble was that the authorities refused to issue the necessary exit permits, yet they made us report each week to Gestapo headquarters where they bullied and threatened and humiliated us for our failure to depart. I was eighteen then and my way of handling the frustration was to go on binges of fanatical housecleaning. When this failed, I took more extreme measures. One day I went to the beauty parlor and had my hair cut within one inch of my scalp. "Something's got to happen," I explained to my horrified mother, "or I'll go out of my mind." Well, I was back to that again, and now I kept busy fretting over hospital regulations and fighting the doctors.

Manipulating the doctors, psyching them out, interpreting them and their recommendations—these absorbing occupations took most of my attention. In dealing with a complex disease like a brain tumor, one is in an area where it is difficult for the layman to make judgments or evaluate the judgments of others. I understand only too well the pitfalls of operating outside of one's own limited field of competence, but now there was no choice. My approach was to provide a team of experts, let them arrive at a collective judgment and insist that they interpret it honestly and openly to Carl and me. But the doctors frequently disagreed and in rather crucial areas I disagreed with them, so the burden of my responsibility became increasingly greater.

Dr. Goldman saw Carl daily and put him through the routine neurological tests. He was young and had an arrogant, offhand manner which irritated Carl quite unduly. He always seemed to be in a hurry when he was in the room, kept answering calls on an air call he carried in his coat pocket and which kept paging him on the average of once every five minutes. He was quite uncommunicative and kept his explanations to a minimum. When I called him from the nursing station phone in an effort to get more complete information from him, he was difficult to reach, made me wait endlessly and then had little to say. I had the impression that he treated me with contempt, perhaps because I am a woman.

One day Carl, who is usually the most patient of men, snapped at him during one of the usual air call interruptions: "Turn that damn thing off when you're in here."

Startled, Dr. Goldman complied. "I'm sorry if it annoys you, but I'm on call."

"The five minutes you're in this room you're supposed to be on call just for me," Carl insisted. "It annoys me a lot."

After Dr. Goldman left, Carl told me he wanted him off the case. "I can't stand him. He treats me like a thing, not a person."

He seemed really agitated and since both Danny and I shared his feelings I decided to speak to Dr. Wolbrenner about it. As the internist he was in charge of coordinating the case and it was he who had put Goldman on in the first place.

74

His response surprised me. "You're not reading him right. True, he's got no bedside manner, but he cares terribly much for his patients. Besides, he's a sort of genius."

"He sure doesn't come across that way. He upsets Carl. What do we need him for, anyway? All he does is the routine tests each day."

"We'll be needing him later." Wolbrenner was thoughtful. "Can't you just accept him on my judgment? . . ."

"Not really. I made clear from the start that the most important thing is for Carl to be treated like a human being. Can't we call in somebody else?"

"Certainly, if you wish." Dr. Wolbrenner became strictly professional. "There are three other neurologists I would consider appropriate choices. How about Dr. Murray?"

Dr. Murray, as I later joked to Carl, turned out to be the same thing in WASP. He was stiff, very authoritative and talked to Carl in meaningless stock phrases appropriate to a fairly bright twelve-year-old. He was in total agreement with Dr. Goldman's diagnosis and treatment recommendations and Carl and I disliked him so much that putting him on the case was out of the question.

Dr. Wolbrenner was rather amused by this turn of events. "Well, what next? Shall I try someone else in the department?"

"Maybe."

"Look, Dr. Murray is a perfectly competent man, but he is a passionate yachtsman. Also, as you noticed, stiff and old-fashioned in style. The main thing with him, if Carl should ever need him on a weekend, forget it. Nothing moves him in from his yacht. The next best guy has a lovely bedside manner, but you can't get him on the phone when you need him. Now, Dave Goldman is accessible, day or night and always. He is really involved. Where we may be going, this may be a lot more important than his bedside manner. Why don't we just stay with him?"

I reluctantly agreed. "Where we may be going" had an ominous ring; obviously he knew things I did not know and did not really want to know. After I discussed it with Carl he decided: "Let's keep him on. I'll handle him."

It turned into a kind of challenge for Carl. Possibly because of a conversation he had had with Wolbrenner, Goldman seemed to be making something of an effort to be friendly at his next visit. Carl responded by trying to charm him. That went over like wet plaster. Still, the air call was never again turned on while he was in the room.

For the next few weeks Carl tried various approaches. Goldman slipped back into his old briskness. Finally, Carl began to talk about his own work, making comparisons between being a neurologist and a film editor. This led to a brief but animated conversation. What a contrast to Wolbrenner and Ambrose, to the lovely team of orthopedists who made long chatty visits! Over the weeks, we established a sort of respectful, businesslike etiquette, the essence of which was that we had forced Dr. Goldman to notice Carl as a person, even if Goldman maintained quite clearly that he did not care to get personally involved with him.

My own relationship with Dr. Goldman continued to be the worst with any of the doctors. I tried to get him to be more considerate of my time and not make me wait each time for phone calls and conferences. I explained that I had a full-time job, that I was a professional woman and carried a lot of responsibility. This cut no ice. He was unimpressed and uncooperative. There were periods when the only way I could or would communicate with him was through one of the other doctors in charge. Throughout, he remained efficient and thoroughly professional. I focused a lot of unexpressed rage on him. I know now that what was enacted during those weeks was an altogether different scenario than that which was openly expressed.

Dr. Wolbrenner's recommendation to keep Dr. Goldman on the case I consider now to have been one of the two best decisions made in the case. The other one was to select Dr. Ambrose as the surgeon. There came a time when Carl and I put all our trust in Dr. Goldman and began to see him as he really is—a brilliant, dedicated scientist who deeply cares for every single one of his patients. Our relationship with him and his with us developed and shifted and was, at the end, one of deep mutual respect. The process by which the dying and their families adjust to the doctors who are in charge of their lives is complex and sometimes painful. The way I now see it, I was struggling to accept the cruelty and irrationality of the entire experience and worked at this consciously. What I did not know and could not then face was my anger, my rage, my sense of being robbed and cheated and persecuted. Dr. Goldman provided me with a focus for that anger, and fighting him was a way for me to release my feelings. He contributed to this unwittingly, by his seeming insensitivity and his inflexible response to our distress. But if it had not been him, it would have had to be someone else. The patient and his family have to react somehow to the disaster that has struck them so unfairly and overwhelmingly. If there had not been a Dr. Goldman, I would have invented him.

From the very onset of Carl's illness the question had arisen whether to stay on my job or to take a leave of absence from the college. As it happened, my usually quite demanding work load of teaching and counseling students was much increased that spring and summer by lecture engagements connected with the publication of my last book. In fact, publication day was the very day on which I was told Carl had a brain tumor. My first reaction had been to drop everything and take up an unceasing vigil at the hospital. Carl firmly decided against that and insisted that I not only stay on my job, but that I keep all previously arranged publicity interviews and lecture dates. This was easier said than done and I found myself moving through these activities in a half-conscious daze, but it obviously meant a lot to Carl. He had always been very supportive of my work, for its own sake and because he knew how much it meant to me. Now he took inordinate pride in everything pertaining to the new book. He listened to my several interviews on his portable radio, he displayed the reviews prominently on his night table and showed copies of the book to all the doctors and nurses. It was his way of continuing his old role and assuring himself of the continuity of life—at least mine, if not his.

I soon learned that working was essential to my own mental health. I gained strength for the long pull by being away from the hospital a few hours each day. Quite apart from financial concerns and the obligations owed to others, to keep some contact with healthy, normal people and especially with the young became more and more of a necessity for me.

There was some social pressure on me to make an opposite decision. The worst conversation of this kind I can remember was with my own physician, a woman doctor whose opinion I greatly respected. When I came for one of my routine checkups, she found me run down and nervous. She knew about Carl's situation and understood the medical picture fully. "You should quit working right now," she advised me in her brisk, professional manner. "Rent a house in the country, get a nurse and a housekeeper and devote the next few months to taking care of your husband. It's going to be a full-time job."

"I don't think I could make it without my work. Besides, Carl would never agree."

"Nonsense," she said with authority. "That kind of decision is not up to him now. You can't go on like this, you'll break down."

"I think I'm more likely to break down if all I have is nursing and the sickness," I mumbled defensively, wondering if perhaps she was right after all.

"You'll never forgive yourself later," she said firmly. I know she meant well and her advice was perhaps quite appropriate for some women, but I have never forgiven her for her certainty and her insensitivity to me as an individual. I did not take her advice and I'm very glad I did not. I did not need anyone loading future guilt on me. Fortunately, some of Carl's doctors and nurses were more supportive of my solution and encouraged me to lead as normal a life as I could. In order to clarify my own mind I tried to imagine what Carl—or any man—would do, if I were the patient. Obviously, it would not occur to him, nor would anyone urge him, to give up his work in order to devote himself to nursing me. This role seems to be considered more appropriate to a woman. "Remember you're a professional," Carl had always said to me whenever I had had such conflicts in the past. To him, being a professional carried high connotations of obligation, commitment and craftsmanship. Act like a professional first, not like a woman first. Remembering this helped me make my decision and stick to it.

Carl's postsurgery recovery had been proceeding so well, the doctors thought I might be able to take him home even before the full course of his cobalt radiation was completed. These treatments could be done three times a week on an outpatient basis, provided I could get him to the hospital. Since this would have to be done during my working hours, it meant finding a nurse able and willing to drive a car.

I consulted the young social worker at the hospital who had earlier offered her services to me. She was very kind and eager to be helpful, but neither she nor the charitable agencies concerned with cancer care could offer any help in obtaining private nursing services. Did I have any financial problem? I said I expected to be able to take care of expenses through insurance and savings. She wondered if I were quite realistic in estimating what the problems might be. Her advice was to put my husband in a nursing home right now, so that he might be entitled to staying there "later." Later. This common euphemism for the terminal stage of a terminal illness had already become familiar. It expressed quite precisely the embarrassment and diffidence people had when dealing with the problems of the dying.

"I expect to keep him home to the end," I told the social worker, who received the information with some hostility. I was obviously not responding according to her expectations. Perhaps I did not realize that I would be faced with a serious problem "later." Because of an acute shortage of hospital beds, voluntary hospitals made it a policy to admit only acute cases. The chronically ill and especially terminal patients (she seemed to have considerable difficulty with that word) were sent to nursing homes, but most of these would not admit patients in the terminal stage unless they had been in residence in the home earlier. For that reason it would be advisable for me to select a nursing home at this time.

I considered the suggestion preposterous and assured her I would not agree to institutionalizing my husband while he was conscious.

"In that case there is nothing I can do for you," she said with some asperity and handed me a list of nursing homes for possible future reference.

The doctors did not wish to advise me on the subject of future care and were quite evasive when I tried to get them to tell me about the likely course of the illness. This was difficult, if not impossible to predict. "Play it by ear," Dr. Ambrose advised, "one week at a time." For the immediate future it was sensible to take Carl home and try to find a good RN. For what period of time? I was asking the impossible. Three to six months, going by the statistics. But the statistics included those who lived longer and those who lived shorter.

Such conversations, unthinkable under ordinary circumstances, had become quite ordinary, and I was able to conduct them with detachment and to the exclusion of any feeling. But my anxiety focused on concrete problems which I pursued doggedly. Did the doctors think it possible and realistic for me to plan to *keep* Carl at home? They would not discuss it. My concern was premature; it depended on circumstances; play it by ear.

After several such frustrating interviews I finally did find someone to give me a straight answer. Bill Rothstein, the neurosurgical resident who had assisted at the operation and who had been taking a great personal interest in Carl, was willing to give me specific facts. He was young enough not to have acquired the self-protective postures of the older doctors; besides, he had convictions on the subject of the rights of patients.

The reason no one could or would make definite predictions, he explained, was that a brain tumor might grow in any direction. Depending on the area affected, anything could happen. No two cases were ever alike. It was best not to try and anticipate. "You've been on this floor long enough to see the variety of possibilities," he added.

Yes, indeed, and every one of them dreadful. "Perhaps he'll lose consciousness," I said.

"Possibly." But that possibility would only compound the nursing problems. On the basis of experience, the progression of the disease would bring spreading paralysis. Hemiplegia or paraplegia—if that happened home care would be very difficult. It would require round-the-clock attendance, possibly even two people at a time, in order to move the patient in and out of bed. There might be need for fairly sophisticated equipment, not to speak of the supervision of a doctor. Even if I could manage to cover the nursing situation, getting a doctor to make house calls might prove impossible.

"True," I said stubbornly, "but it could be managed. As long as I know what to expect."

"You're not considering the real problem," he pointed out. "That's you and your children. You might be able to solve all the practical problems, but you'll find it impossible to take, day after day. It's very hard. A lot of relatives start out with the best of intentions and in a few weeks or months they come here and beg us to take the patient back because it's too much for them."

"That may be. But I'll still have to try."

"Why?" he asked. Nobody else had bothered to ask that question.

"Because a person has a right to die the way he has lived. His own way, in his own environment, maybe even in his own time. To put him in an institution seems to me like abandoning him. I couldn't ever forgive myself for it."

"I believe that too," Dr. Rothstein said quietly. "I wish more people did. If it were my father—" He let his voice trail off. I felt deeply grateful for this response on a personal level, especially since I had already learned most people responded with embarrassment and discomfort to my insistence on opposing institutionalized death.

"You know, you might just do it," he said suddenly. "I'll help you. Just don't blame yourself if you can't carry it off all the way." We became friends that moment and have been ever since. He had made a serious promise and he kept it. As time went on, I would be needing more such allies and, miraculously, I found them.

Meanwhile, my priority was finding a nurse. I spoke to each of the very good nurses who had taken care of Carl in the hospital, but there were no takers. The better trained a nurse is, the less likely she is to go on a home-care case where she has to deal not only with medical problems, but also with the patient's relatives. It takes a nurse who will place human concern above self-interest. I finally found one nurse who considered taking the job when I emphasized that I would be out of the house practically all the time she was there. She would be in complete charge. Carole Tabor was a lively, highly intelligent nurse who took pride in her professional competence. She was interested in the physical therapy aspect of the case and had become quite attached to Carl, because of his determined fight for rehabilitation. She said she liked my attitude and especially the fact that I kept on working. I wanted to know if she had ever handled a terminal case.

She had, and was honest enough to say that she had found it very difficult, but it was a challenge a good nurse had to meet.

"I've made up my mind to keep my husband home. All the way. I need a nurse who will help me. Can you promise to stay?"

Carole thought it over for a while and said she respected my decision a good deal. She would stay till the end of the year, at least. She would *try* to stay all the way, which was the best she could give me by way of a promise.

I thought it was a lot.

After two "weekend-pass" visits, Carole and I brought Carl home on June 3, 1972. Carl was in high spirits and began to take charge of his affairs. He answered the phone and planned the visitors' schedule. His daily routine was as rigorous as it had been in the hospital. It took the full-time attention of his nurse and a good deal of my time as well. It formed the basic pattern of our life during the following months; only it would later become much more cumbersome.

We came quickly to accept his current status as normal, regarding deviations from it as "illness." He dressed each morning, afternoon and evening in street clothes. He ate all his meals at the table, except when he was "ill." He had a full bath daily; during this earlier period he was still able to take a shower. He attempted to shave himself with his left hand and the electric razor, but finally permitted the nurse or me to do it for him. It was typical of him that during his entire illness he never let a day go by without being shaved and properly groomed. At night he had a rubdown and massage before going to sleep. He worked on rehabilitating his right leg by doing strengthening exercises for half an hour twice a day, lifting weights with his legs, flexing, pushing. He did these same exercises under supervision at the hospital twice a week, prior to his radiation therapy. He walked for short periods at least three times a day and spent fifteen minutes to an hour outdoors. To improve his hand, he exercised each muscle and joint of fingers, wrist, elbow and shoulder morning and night. Some of this was active exercise, some of it passive. Because the paralyzed limbs tended to become edemic, engorged with fluid, the nurse and I massaged the hand and foot for fifteen minutes at a time several times a day. In addition to all this Carl practiced finger movements with his right hand and writing and drawing with his left hand. He learned to help himself in the many routines of daily living: feed himself with the left hand, adjust his clothes, dial the telephone.

He was easily fatigued, took several naps a day and found conversation for more than short periods quite tiring. We kept busy, usually too busy to see friends during the day. Evenings were for visitors.

They came faithfully and cheerfully, two to four a day for eighteen months. There would have been more if we could have accepted them. They brought food, flowers, films they were working on, play scripts. They read to him, asked his advice on their various artistic projects, discussed the news with him and kept him closely tied to all the usual concerns of his normal working life. They found innumerable ways to express their love and affection for him, to distract him and entertain him and to help me. Carl found a way of expressing what these visits meant to him. It was his own idea and he worked hard at drafting the letter, signing it with his left hand and preparing the mailing list. We sent it to everyone who had helped us during those months and were surprised that the mailing list included nearly seventy persons. This was the letter we sent:

June 5, 1972

Dear friend:

I would like to respond to all the many people who have sent me messages and tokens of support;

to those who have tried to telephone me;

to those who have visited me and to those who have tried to visit me and could not do so because of my limited ability to have visitors;

to the people who have brought me dinner because of my low tolerance for hospital food;

to all of you who have stood by me, by Gerda and Danny in the worst hours and days;

I would like to respond to all of you, but at this time I'm unable to write to you personally.

I would like to say that this outpouring of support, friendship, concern and love—something I have never experienced before in my life—has been most touching and meaningful to me. It has helped me in pulling out of this very bad trip.

Even though I am now out of the hospital, I have a long ways to go toward recovery. In these difficult days your friendship has been overwhelmingly real. It is much needed now and in the future.

Thank you. *Carl*

Our friends were very touched by his letter and told us so. I hope it was adequate in expressing our gratitude and I fear it was not, for as our needs increased our demands on our friends increased. There would come a time when our needs were so great, our demands would be unrealistic and wholly inconsiderate. Already, I subordinated all considerations of friendship or courtesy to Carl's needs, which seemed to me primary. One of my problems was to curb the overly enthusiastic visitors who, inspired by Carl's spirited fight for recovery and perhaps acting out their own psychic needs, spurred him on to greater efforts in the mistaken belief they were helping him. As it was, he was pushing too hard and suffered from stress, exhaustion and insomnia. It was during this period I began to play the role of "protective dragon," shooing people out of the room, intervening in their conversation, at times offending friends in order to protect Carl.

While some of this behavior was sensible and necessary, part of it reflected the deep uneasiness I felt over the continuing deception of all but a handful of friends as to the hopeless prognosis of his case. When I had first agreed to hold off telling Carl the truth about his condition, I had decided that it would be impossible to carry it off if too many people knew the truth. I stuck to a cover story: a tumor had successfully been removed and there was hope for recovery, even for recovery from the paralysis of the hand and arm. I had promised the doctors to wait about speaking to Carl until radiation therapy was over and I had promised myself to wait until Carl gave a sign of wanting to know the truth.

He showed no such sign in those first weeks at home. On the contrary, he projected a cheerful, positive attitude and demanded the same from those around him. We hardly talked of his condition, except to record improvements. He kept me at a distance and never spoke of his feelings.

Since his surgery he had difficulty focusing his eyes for reading and so I took to reading to him each night before he went to sleep. I tried to read poetry, which he had always enjoyed, but he rejected everything that was "deep." The books we read were *Winnie-the-Pooh*, *Alice in Wonderland*, German fairy tales. Short stories proved to be better suited to his attention span than longer works, so we read a lot of Chekhov stories, Guy de Maupassant and a few selected classics. Someone brought a book of Malamud stories. I began to read the first one out loud before I realized that it dealt with death and dying. I wanted to stop but Carl made me read on. It was a grim story, as were most of the stories in that volume, all dealing with the edges of experience, with hidden terrors, loneliness and alienation. We read them all and then began on another volume. Several of these stories we read repeatedly; it was the only way in which Carl was able to get in touch with his new reality. Sometimes when we had finished he pressed my fingers between his with his good left hand, then pushed me away. The signals were clear: he was displacing the truth and did not want to hear it.

So I had to wait with my revelations. I had to dissemble and hold my tongue and somehow deal with my own guilt feelings about violating what had been our prior agreement on handling such situations. Part of my reason for wanting to keep Carl at home had been to allow him a choice. From knowing him as I did, I had no doubt that he would not want to live in severe impairment. But what was that? He was already crippled and might soon be paralyzed on his entire right side. Wheelchair. When he had first come home from surgery, I had ordered a wheelchair together with the hospital bed, so as to simulate hospital conditions. I carefully explained to him that we would use the wheelchair only for longer excursions outdoors, so that his range of motion would be improved. Or, if he preferred, we could use it only in the apartment, to save him from exertion. Carl had angrily refused to try it, even to have it in his room, and insisted that I return it that day. Still, I thought, if he really needed it he might put up with a wheelchair. But loss of speech? Loss of sight? If he knew these were coming, I had little doubt he would prefer to die sooner. Long ago, during our friend's terminal illness, we had discussed these questions and his statements had been unequivocal.

So I had to prepare myself. I tried to arrange the circumstances of his life so that he would retain the choice each healthy adult has. But how, and to what extent, could I involve myself? Would I have the courage to help him?

Such thoughts were constantly in my mind, yet I could not pursue them very far. My first barrier was reached very quickly—it always came down to telling him the truth about his condition. Once he knew the full truth, he might decide to end his life. In that sense, the longer I deceived him, the better. Precisely here was my moral dilemma. I was already part of the conspiracy of silence the doctors had advised. Suppose I waited too long and by the time he learned the truth he could no longer move on his own? Or what if he could no longer speak and tell me what he wanted—

I stopped there, over and over again. Perhaps, I told myself, all this is only selfishness. Perhaps this care and nursing is more than you bargained for and that's why you can think such terrible thoughts. . . . But I knew this was not true. I wanted him alive, I wanted him with me no matter how bad it was. I knew it would be so much worse without him. I tried to think meaning into that phrase, without him, and I could not. All I knew is that I honestly and truly did not want to live without him. I went through that many times—the children, my work, my friends, there were so many things that should have meaning for me. Yet in all those months I got no further than that my life would end when his life ended, even if I should physically survive.

The only happy moments and hours I had were being in the room where he lay, being able to see him, touch him, do this or that little thing for him. . . . The thought of doing without that was like looking down the black hole of an empty mine shaft and feeling repelled and drawn to it at the same time. There was no doubt in my mind and feelings that I wanted to keep him alive, desperately. I was conspiring with the rest of the world and in a sense with Carl's assistance to keep the truth as far away as possible. Yet I was convinced then, and am convinced now, that dimly Carl already knew and was trying to protect himself and me from the change that would come into our relationship once the words were spoken.

Seen in retrospect, these weeks were the "good" weeks, but apparently for me they were really quite bad. While Carl was still in the hospital I had begun to have a severe pain in my face, running from the right eye to the upper jaw. I tried to ignore it and took painkillers, then consulted my dentist who diagnosed it as an infected tooth, which he treated with massive doses of antibiotics. The pain got worse; the antibiotics did not touch the infection and my dentist decided the tooth would have to be extracted.

The dental surgeon to whom he referred me was a kindly, elderly man. He did not hold out much hope for saving the tooth, but thought root-canal work should be tried.

I explained that I had no time nor energy for extended treatment and wanted the tooth pulled at once. As I began to describe my situation, I suddenly fell into an uncontrollable fit of crying, the worst I had had till then. I was past embarrassment; probably the pain and the annoyance at this stupid and irrelevant intrusion, the realization of my own vulnerability, made me finally let go. The dentist gave me time, sympathy and a tranquilizer, but he also spoke firmly about my needing to pay some attention to my own physical condition.

For the next months I went twice a week to have root-canal work done and to cry when the physical pain offered a handy excuse. Somehow, being a patient in a doctor's chair gave me a chance to let go and I found I felt better after each of these painful sessions. The work progressed badly; eventually the tooth had to be extracted and bridgework had to be done.

During this time I caught a cold, just an ordinary cold to which, under normal circumstances, I would pay little attention. However, a patient in Carl's condition is very vulnerable to infection and the nurse impressed me with the need for protecting him. I wore a mask when I came near him and tried to cure myself by going to bed early and taking large doses of vitamin C. One night, lying alone in our king-size bed and suffering the misery of a cold plus toothache, I suddenly experienced the full extent of my loneliness. It was such a small illness, such a minor discomfort, measured against what Carl was experiencing, but it was the first time in our married life he was not there to bring me a cup of tea and say a word of encouragement. Not only was he not there, but he never again would be there, no matter what my distress. I lay in bed and let myself understand what this meant, fully and horribly. I let myself sink into the misery, not trying to shield myself from it, speaking it out loud in my mind so I might understand it and take it in and perhaps, in doing so, learn to sustain it. Then a second horror took hold of me: what if I got worse, bronchitis, pneumonia—who would take care of him? How would I be able to manage the precarious system of care I had instituted for him, if anything went wrong with me?

Interesting, how the practical nightmare suppressed and supplanted the larger horror. That night I came to terms with my new situation: not only did I have no one I could lean on for support, but I was now the sole support of Carl's precarious existence. I would have to take better care of my health in the future and I would have to make plans for contingencies. After that night's crisis I took some practical steps. I arranged with Danny that he would substitute for me if I got sick or needed a day's rest away from home. We worked out some trial runs to teach him all he needed to know about Carl's care. He proved to be a wonderful nurse and companion and Carl learned to accept help from him without apparent difficulty. He came at least once a week and later on took over about once a month to give me a weekend off. This simple step toward sharing responsibility proved to be as good for him as it was for Carl and me.

I arranged for a practical nurse to come regularly for a late afternoon shift, in order to relieve myself of the necessity of preparing dinner and giving nursing care after I got home from work. Another step was to hire a weekend nurse and try to find someone who would be a reliable and steady replacement should Carole be unavailable. This was a most difficult problem and one which I never could adequately solve. Finally, I saw our lawyer and made some financial arrangements, which would secure Carl's full and adequate care at home, in case anything happened to me.

My experience with the infected tooth and with my cold also reinforced in me the decision to accept professional help and psychiatric counseling and to admit to myself that I could not possibly pull this alone. Of all the difficult decisions I had to take, this was perhaps the most difficult. It was also the most helpful.

July 1972

FOCAL SEIZURE

*Seizures are electrical impulses gone
wild in the overloaded circuits of the
brain, causing muscles to tremble and
twitch uncontrollably*

*there is, they say, no pain,
but the eyes of the victims
say otherwise*

*look in the mirror, love,
right side sagging, idiot
child, guileless, smiling*

*gamboling lamb, wonder at
absurdity. Sunflecks dance
on the windowsill and*

*cockroaches the size of mice
come out of the walls
in legions*

We made plans, wild, joyous and complex plans. We
have a summer house on the North Shore of Long Island, a shabby, comfortable place on a wooded hill,
near the water. We love it and have spent only happy,
relaxed days there. Every shrub and plant in the garden
was planted by us and has its own personal history for
us. We wanted to spend the summer in Huntington—

the very thought of it filled Carl with hope.

Dr. Ambrose suggested we first try several short day visits. The thirty-minute ride to the hospital had accustomed Carl to car travel and he was well enough to take very short walks. We could break the trip to the island into two periods with a lengthy rest stop in between. I was a little worried about the seven steps leading into the house, but Carl had been taught how to walk stairs in Rehab and was confident he could do it.

We went out there on a Saturday in July, just he and I. Although it fatigued him, he loved the ride. He managed the steps with considerable effort, but also with competence. As soon as he got into the house, he went to bed and fell asleep at once. When he awoke and realized where he was, he smiled delightedly.

We spent a very quiet day. Carl mostly sat on the porch, looking into the trees and watching the birds. In the evening we drove to the beach, and sitting in the car with the roof rolled down, he watched the sunset. He slept better than usual that night.

Sunday morning we went to the beach, where Carl sat in a chair by the water, while I took a quick swim. He was not allowed to sit in the direct sun and we protected his head with a cap and a beach umbrella. It was a happy half hour.

After the beach, we usually took a shower in our basement shower room, and we did so that day. It's an old-fashioned stall shower with a wooden bench, which Carl could use quite conveniently. After his shower, just as he was dressing, his right eyelid began to quiver. He called my name and I turned just in time to see a spasm contort the right side of his face. He looked ghastly. I got him to sit down. His eyes were blank with terror; he seemed to be listening inside himself. Then his arm and hands began to shake violently and uncontrollably.

"I'm having a seizure," he said. "Stay with me." My impulse was to hold the twitching hand, but he directed me to hold his other hand. His face twitched once again and then it all stopped. He looked ashen and was weak and seemed like a person in shock.

Everything I had learned about seizures in these months rushed through my mind in a few seconds. Muscle spasms can spread to various parts of the body or recur repeatedly in one part only. They can become so violent that the whole body is involved. The force of such seizures is so great people can break arms or legs without feeling it. As it worsens, the patient may become unconscious, roll his eyes backward, foam at the mouth. This is a grand mal seizure. The immediate danger at that stage is injury from falling or choking by biting or swallowing the tongue. The greater danger, in case of a brain tumor, is that seizures can cause more damage to brain and body function. In case of seizure: See that the patient is in a safe, comfortable, preferably cushioned place. Stay calm and calm him. If it gets into the grand mal stage, place a tongue blade or spoon between his jaws to prevent injury to the tongue and choking. Afterward, make him lie down, keep him warm, call the doctor.

At this moment all this advice seemed preposterous. Carl was sitting half-dressed on a straight chair in a basement bathroom. To get him warm and comfortable I had to get him up a flight of stairs. Impossible. The telephone was upstairs. How could I leave him?

A few minutes after the attack was over, I draped towels around him for warmth and got a beach lounge, on which I made him stretch out. I explained that I would have to leave him briefly in order to get help. He was terrified about being left alone, but it had to be. I raced upstairs, phoned a friend and neighbor and got a blanket. When I returned with it, Carl seemed all right, but said he felt very weak. I stayed with him till the neighbor came, who then kept him company while I called a doctor.

We had a fine arrangement with the hospital for emergencies and, in less than five minutes, I had a neurosurgery resident on the phone. His advice was: get him upstairs, if he can walk. See if there are any other symptoms, such as weakness in any limb. Let him rest and then drive him home to the city, if he seems all right. Double his medicine and call back in an hour. Otherwise, get him to the hospital in an ambulance.

There were no further difficulties and we returned to the city that night. I was badly shaken. It was obvious to me that, if this attack had been any bigger, it would have been a disaster. I simply could not stay at the house alone with Carl. The house was too big; the neighbors were too far away. He could only be out there if there were at least two healthy people in the place. Worse, perhaps the whole trip had been too much for him. Had the physical strain and the psychological excitement caused this attack? Perhaps it was the trip to the beach? The shower? My first response was vague guilt. It must have been something we did; there must be some rational cause which could prevent this from happening in the future. In the coming weeks and months the nurses and I—and to an extent the doctors—pursued the futile course of looking for rational causes. What we were really trying to do was to find a way to control the irrational. If we could only understand what was happening, we could fight effectively. But the cancer in Carl's head—which I had begun to think of very simply and literally as "the monster"—followed no rules understood by science and rationality. It grew, it spread here or there, it retreated, it sent out polyplike fingers into distant parts of the brain, it convulsed nerve tissue into seizuring. We looked for causes, for patterns.

Following that seizure in Huntington, Carl had several falls in which he suddenly pitched forward or backward. It was obvious these were not accidents caused by his coming across some sudden obstacle, but rather incidents indicative of a malfunctioning in his signal system. Increasingly, he showed loss of balance and of space perception. When sitting, he would rock forward or sideways, not quite knowing where his body was. In walking, he would cross one foot over the other, a condition we tried to control by making him aware of each movement he was making. It cost him, during those weeks, enormous effort to go through the simplest motions. He made the effort and it visibly exhausted him and, for days at a time, he showed tiny gains in control. But these would be wiped out, over and over again, by a seizure episode and its consequences.

Within a week after the seizure in Huntington, his balance was so bad he had to be supported by being held by his belt every time he stood up or walked. On July 15 he was unable to walk and fell sideways as he tried to sit up. Dr. Ambrose thought we might be dealing with a drug reaction rather than a progression of tumor pressure. He felt this was an area of treatment in which Dr. Goldman was more competent than he was and proposed to let the neurologist take over this phase of treatment. Accordingly, I called Dr. Goldman and was astonished and gratified to find him willing to make a house call.

It was typical of Dr. Goldman that he would make a house call in Queens, which involved for him perhaps an hour's loss of his precious time, charge what for a specialist was a moderate fee for such a service, prescribe a new course of treatment and yet would evoke in us not only gratitude and confidence in his ability, but outrage and anger. He did this by spending no more than five minutes in the apartment, refusing to sit down while he was there and pronouncing his diagnosis—which turned out to be absolutely correct—a minute after he entered the room and without having spoken a personal word to a patient who was in mental agony, thinking he had finally lost his ability to walk. "It's nothing but Dilantin toxicity," Dr. Goldman declared, ordered Carl to bed for a week, left changed drug orders with the nurse and departed. We had longed for some reassurance and explanation which would permit us to find some perspective toward our multiple problems. The answer was actually implicit in Dr. Goldman's diagnosis. Drug reactions are to be expected when such

massive doses of drugs are used for patient mainte-
nance. Each patient reacts individually and often the
mere substitution of one drug for another will temporarily solve a most vexing problem. Such drug substitutions
must be made gradually and with great care and many
unexpected side effects may occur during such transition periods. Dr. Goldman was very cognizant of all of
these facts, handled the actual medical supervision most
skillfully and effectively, but failed to deal with the anxiety and bewilderment of his patient. It was this fact,
and the fact that he seemed to give no credit or consid-
eration to our intelligence and desire to share in the
management of the illness, which made us feel angry
and disappointed despite our gratitude for his having
made a house call.

As before, our complex relationship with the physi-
cians reflected developing adjustment to the course of
the illness. After the initial shock of surgery and the acceptance of the desperate medical outlook, we had lived
through a brief few weeks of obvious improvement.
Now we entered what I later came to think of as the
"period of the seizures," in which the randomness of
the progression of deterioration became something we
had to learn to deal with. It was a period during which,
within four months and with many ups and downs and
small remissions, there was steady and perceptible deterioration of function. The substitution of one drug for
another, the changes in regime, the various methods of
physical therapy all served to maintain hope and to alle-
viate one minor symptom or another. They did nothing, nor could they be expected to do anything, to affect the actual course of the disease.

But in those early weeks we still entertained the futile
hope for some measure of control. I spent months keeping minute records of my and the nurses' daily observations, hoping to find some pattern or clue as to the fac-
tors causing the seizures. All futile.

"That's why people go to horror movies," my wise
psychiatrist friend observed. "They watch the Blob or

some giant-sized insects attack the world and it makes the horror visual and helps to work out our fear of the unknown. The fact is, there is irrationality in the world and we have to learn to live with it and accept it."

He and Dr. Goldman were the only doctors who took a consistently scientific view, accepting the limitations imposed by medical ignorance. This was, at the beginning, an idea which it was impossible for the patient and his relatives to accept. We took comfort in the futile search for remedies. Dr. Ambrose imposed stringent rules in order to avoid or minimize seizures: no more showers, only sponge baths. No trips to the country. No trips to the beach. Constant attendance and observation of the patient. No mental or emotional excitement.

"None of this will, in my opinion, affect the seizures," Dr. Goldman disagreed with his usual bluntness. "They will occur regardless. You and Mr. Lerner will have to learn to live with them. Let's hope they stay small and do no major damage."

One more reason, at that time, to distrust and dislike Dr. Goldman. How much better to feel that, with solid medical support, we were doing something useful toward prevention and control. And yet, Carl could have enjoyed a summer in the country. He could have lived more fully and normally, perhaps for a shorter time, if we had been willing to accept the inevitable. Instead, by October, I presented Dr. Ambrose with a detailed chart of each seizure since July 9, summarized as follows:

Intervals between seizures since July 9:
10 days; 10; 10; 3; 17; 6; 2; 5; 8; 4; 4; 2; 13; 13; 10; 12; 13; 1; 12; 10; 11; 5.

Dr. Ambrose studied the list carefully, praised me for bringing it in and found it, essentially, useless. For the seizures continued, no matter what we did. They were a constant, ever-present threat which haunted us.

The attacks came at various times: once in a movie, once or twice while there were visitors, several times outdoors, but mostly at home, at rest, in bed. Undoubtedly, there were several during sleep. Carl was terrified by them and the frequency of repetition in no way dimmed his horror. I never could find out quite what his sensation was. It was not pain, but some sort of psychic shock more numbing than pain. What made it truly terrifying to both of us was that over the months every serious deterioration in Carl's condition was preceded by a seizure. Not every seizure brought obvious consequences; in fact, most of them were harmless. But each spread of paralysis followed immediately upon a seizure.

During these months, with minor fluctuations, Carl's gait became more and more unsteady. He worked hard at controlling and retaining his ability to walk, but ever-increasing effort seemed to yield poorer results. First he had to learn to accept that he could not rely on his balance and that he needed to be protected against sudden falls: a cane in his left hand for support; an awareness of the need to walk close to a supporting surface; a person forever at his right side or just slightly behind him in order to grab hold of him in case of need. The threat of seizures led to his having to accept the constant presence of a nurse or companion. This, in many ways, was the hardest to accept for a man who had always been self-reliant and often solitary and who needed, psychically, to have long stretches of silence and aloneness. It was doubly difficult for me, because of my own similar needs and because of my responsibility for providing this steady and reliable supervision. It seemed to me then to have added yet another loss to our many losses: the loss of privacy during the period of our lives together when such privacy seemed most needed and wanted.

Recurrent loss of balance was worsened by increasing muscle weakness in both legs following various seizures. The drugs used in an effort to control the seizures had the effect of making Carl drowsy, temporarily slurring his speech, blurring his alertness. While he seemed to need more and more rest periods during the day, he slept worse and more fitfully during the night. As the steady deterioration inevitably became apparent to him, he became more anxious, which always found expression in insomnia. My medical notes during this period show that there was hardly a night when he was not awake at least twice between 11:00 P.M. and 7:00 A.M. Often he was awake for hours during the night. We still managed with only a day nurse and a part-time evening shift nurse. The going-to-bed routine and the night shift were my responsibility. I slept in his room on a couch and awakened when he did. My memory, which has been very tricky and poor, has closed over those nights: I do not remember anything about them nor do I remember how I managed to get up in the morning and go to work. Sometime during that fall, Carl insisted I sleep in the other room and to convince me to do so he promised to call me when he awoke by ringing an electrical bell, which we installed by his bed. I know he often did not call me and I have a fair perception of what this must have cost him. He struggled with great strength and dignity to retain a measure of his ability to be a living, giving person. I accepted his self-denial out of necessity. I had already learned that I could not hope to pull this if I tried to be heroic. I needed what sleep I could get.

The seizures were a most refined form of torture for us, because of their randomness and destructive potential. For me, there was the added horror of knowing precisely what they might bring next: recurring paralysis of the right side, spread of paralysis to the left side, facial paralysis, loss of speech, blindness (not likely in his case), deafness (not likely), paralysis of the swallowing apparatus. Slow death by slow torture.

Carl did not, fortunately, know the precise sequence of possible or expected horrors. I never thought that truthfulness need include this. What good could it possibly do for him to make images in the mind of the next stage and the next? He knew enough, instinctively, or perhaps from signals from within his body. As always, he followed medical direction faithfully as long as he believed in it. Sometime in December, when the seizures had gotten more frequent and had resulted in increasing weakness in the legs, he lost faith in the efforts at control. He expressed it once, when we talked about taking him to the movies. He wanted to go. I pointed out that the last time he had been to the movies, he had had a seizure at the theater. Maybe it would be better not to risk that again so soon?

"Oh, fuck the seizures," he said, grinning. It was not language he usually used.

The nurse came in the next morning with a cute little cartoon she had drawn, showing Snoopy doing a jig. "Fuck the seizures," was his message. Carl was delighted with it, hung it up where all visitors could see it and derived comfort from this small gesture of cosmic defiance.

Fuck the seizures. We did the best we could. In the end, they got us. But we tried.

July 1972–August 1973

They have eaten our lives

They came to help, friendliness their disguise.
Others we hire; these deliver opinions,
judgements,
stones cast upon us who
have asked for bread.
We hire charity, rent
concern by the hour plus carfare,
a percentage to the agency
sending us
locusts.

The air is theirs; the rugs keep
their perfume, the curtains
hold the smell of their cigarettes.
Their noise surrounds us:
whispers, trained footsteps.
Conversation,
our words fit
their mouths, their ears.
We have tailored our lives,
what is left of our lives,
to fill their
empty
spaces.

They have engulfed us,
an avalanche of helpers
slowly advancing.   We are
gasping, swallowing strange air.
The space between us, that delicate
delight of balance, shared
silence
stuffed with their clatter,
their grasping arms, their
rented
smiles.

105

Interdependence and sharing—we had to learn it and learn it fast. Carl, whose losses were so total, brutal and final, was forced into dependence from the moment he entered the hospital. Everything now came to him through others. Instinctively, he grasped for every hand he could reach, transforming his increasing helplessness into a proud and giving acceptance of interdependence which enriched the giver more than the receiver. My dependency was different, because I constantly struggled with choices. I have never been good at giving over to others what I could do for myself; surely, as I know now, this was a failure of trust on my part, not theirs. In those first months I thought I could still go on as before, managing everything efficiently and alone—super-woman-juggler-on-a-tightrope—but things were long out of control already. I was still struggling to keep this dying as something belonging to the two of us, something we would fashion together as we had fashioned our marriage, something for me to keep and survive by—but it did not happen that way. It could not happen that way and the one who had to learn it was me.

To be helpless and in need before one's children— that was the profoundest experience of them all. We had thought ourselves such enlightened parents in staying clear of our children's adulthood, being available to them when they needed us, but trying not to interfere with them. Trying above all not to make demands on them. We probably did not succeed; parents seldom do with their noblest intentions. Our unspoken expectations, excessive and greedy like those of most parents, must have come across to them in unspoken ways. We often talked about how we did not ever want our children to do anything for us because it was a duty. Somehow it did not occur to us that they would always freely give us their help from love.

I had waited for weeks to allow Danny—who had always been ready to do so—to take part in Carl's physical care. My fear was that this most obvious sign of his helplessness would further hurt and embarrass Carl. Yet, when Dan took over his care that first weekend I left for the country, Carl accepted it with unselfconscious innocence. There were times, later, when Dan lifted and carried his father, and the sight of it, sad as it was, was beautiful because of the natural, loving way in which both of them handled it. Dan has his father's marvelous sense of humor and somehow he brought out what was left of joy and humor in Carl. The two of them were having a good time together, no matter what their activity was.

The problem of Stephanie continued to weigh on me. I had never been dishonest with my daughter in her life and I felt very conflicted about the continuing deception we were practicing in the name of protection. She was not fully restored in health herself, yet she had begun with considerable courage to make a new life in Holland. Telling her the truth now would force her into making difficult decisions from which I had wanted, instinctively, to shield her as long as possible. If she decided to come to visit, it would mean upheaval and stress and pain in her life; if she decided not to come to visit, why tell her the truth and add to her agony? I had experienced this situation during the war, when my mother was terminally ill and I could not be near her and all I knew came to me in letters. It seemed horrible to have to impose the same nightmare on my daughter.

As for protecting Carl, I had come to think for some time that the doctors' advice was wrong and my judgment worse in accepting it. Carl had been seizuring wildly for weeks, with good cause and without it, with strain and without it, and we had learned to accept this condition. More and more, I felt that nobody could and should be protected from the truth. Risks would have to be taken if life were to be "meaningful." The need to protect Carl from strain and Stephanie from upheaval would have to be weighed against her right to know. Whatever came of it just had to happen. She had a right to make her own choice in this and I had to face fully what it means not to take responsibility for another person's life, not even for the child I had carried and loved and cared for, and who now was an adult. Once having come to this conviction, Danny and I talked it over and we agreed that he should phone Stephanie, instead of my writing her; we thought it would make it a little easier for her. She took a plane to New York two hours after Danny called her, as I expected she would—never hesitating and never thinking of the complications it made in her own life. She left the new friends, the work, the man she loved, and came and stayed with us to the end and that was one of the most important and positive acts of her life. It was immensely important to me, also, meaningful in many ways, some of which I am still exploring and perceiving.

As for Carl, we told him she was coming home only after she had landed at the airport. He accepted the news with a simplicity that must have come from a deep inner need. I will never forget the look of joy and relief on his face when she entered the room. If there had ever been any tension, it was wiped away and forgotten and nothing needed to be explained. From then on there was nothing that gave him greater comfort and peace than to be with his children. Perhaps the dying need most of all a close tie with the next generation, their continuity, their heirs. There was something sweet and infinitely tender in this relationship. Carl had never been able to express his love and caring in words. Now it was all there, open and vulnerable in the way he shared his pain, his sorrow and his deep inner strength with his children. They in turn, gently and persistently, began to be felt. Their father was dying; this was their tragedy as well as ours; they wanted and needed to share in it fully. I slowly advanced to the recognition that not only did they need this, but I did as well. The way Carl accepted his children caring for him without false pride and undue fuss showed me the way. I am convinced it was one of the best things we as parents ever did for them. We came very much closer through this ordeal as a family than we had ever been.

Other kinds of dependency had to be learned. As Carl was imprisoned in his paralyzed and inefficient body, so I was imprisoned in his illness and my dependency on paid help. In many ways I was fortunate. I had a housekeeper who stayed on through it all, a kind immigrant woman who had lived over thirty years in this country but still retained the basic values of her peasant background: the dying belong at home; the dying have rights. The mother of five children, she came three times a week, cooked, cleaned, scrubbed and suffered throughout the incredible turmoil of running a hospital in a five-room city apartment with a kitchen the size of a small closet. She quietly incorporated Carl's illness into the network of her family caring.

For me, the crucial person was the day nurse. If I could find a reliable day nurse I could keep my job, secure in knowing that Carl would have intelligent companionship in addition to reliable medical care. It was a tall order. We were lucky twice. Carole was everything one could hope for and she stayed through that first summer. Then she left because she had been offered a challenging job she had long been trying to get, a job combining nursing with medical administration which she felt she could not in good conscience refuse. Carl accepted that, although he hated to lose her. I thought, despite her protests, that the real reason she was leaving was that she had been drawn into that error fatal to good nursing—she had lost her professional detachment. Now it was too painful for her to stay through the terminal stage and thus, perhaps, she was right in leaving. At the time, I simply felt abandoned and bitter. I know that by our very existence Carl and I were confronting each person who came near us with the need to define his or her attitude toward death. One should probably be tolerant of the burden this places on most people, but I had no strength left for tolerance. Bitterness and anger were helpful to me in mobilizing my resources and so I hoarded them. Carole did a great thing, though—she helped to find her successor.

Sharon was young, pretty, exuberant. Different from Carole, she was an excellent nurse in her own way, and proud of her skills. I thought during our first interview that she was too immature, too robust and energetic, to cope with the often tedious demands of the job, but the phrase with which she replied, when I asked her about making a long-range commitment, appealed to me quite irrationally. "I'm a faithful nurse," she said and I understood that that was her own definition of commitment.

Sharon very quickly developed an adoring attitude toward Carl, which seemed to me to be simply an adolescent crush. I watched Carl feed her admiration, flirt with her in a way that seemed to me both pathetic and appalling, charm her as he had charmed the rest of the personnel at the hospital. I could not be angry with him for doing this, but I could resent her. I worked hard at controlling that resentment and I hope I succeeded. Often, it was the ordeal of the hospital all over again: Carl rejecting me and pushing me aside, while praising everything Sharon did for him. Just to get what he needed, I then thought spitefully. Now, as I think of it, it seems to me quite remarkable that in those last terrible months he still had the vitality and energy left to build a new relationship, to project himself as a person in relation to another person. He was giving something to Sharon, something that lasted beyond his lifetime. To have been able to do so is really quite wonderful.

As she had promised, Sharon stayed with us to the end, lending us her energy and vitality to do daily battle against our state of horror. It often seemed then that the moment her young, vigorous presence pervaded the room, death would have to withdraw. It must have seemed that way to Carl and I understand why he needed to cling to her. Yet it was bitter for me to have to deal with all this. Far too often I resented the time she spent with Carl while I was working, the obvious truth in her assertion that, because she was "strong as an ox," she could help him better in his daily activities than I could. True, and I had a bad back and could not lift him or hold him the way she could and he knew it and let me know it. It pains me to have to set down in honesty my confused feelings, which often amounted to nothing loftier than jealousy. In many ways I made Sharon a scapegoat for my despair, as I made Dr. Goldman a scapegoat. But such perversion of good sense, such ambivalence, such anger at helplessness and dependency are also part of the process of dying. With all that, I fully trusted Sharon's skill, her professional knowledge and her good judgment. Our relationship was rocky: at times full of tension, at other times earnestly respectful and understanding on both sides. It was the measure of the dependency into which the three of us were locked. Carl and I needed Sharon. She needed our need of her. In retrospect, I consider it our great good luck that she came into our lives and stayed with us the way she did.

Whenever she went on vacation or during weekends, I really learned to appreciate what we had in Sharon. It seemed I was to be engaged in an everlasting quest for a reliable, steady weekend nurse, for vacation replacements, late afternoon and night shifts. I used every agency available; I paid more than top salaries; I kept taxis on call; I offered all kinds of bonuses. We lived through the usual assortment of incompetent or unreliable people: those too old or ill trained to be employable in the hospitals; practicals with little training; others who, despite the job specification, never intended to stay for more than a week. Jehovah's Witnesses sent us a succession of gentle West Indians, male and female, who were kindly, neat, sometimes untrained, often too lively. A brain-injured patient is incredibly sensitive to noise and touch and Carl's tolerance for making adjustments was extremely low. We lost many a potentially good nurse, because he could not live through the first days of training. He became irritable and uncooperative and frightened some of these good women so they would not come near him. He did not give a damn for my problem in supplying him with nurses and expected them simply to be there, which certainly was his right. The problems of staffing this private hospital were enormous and incessant.

There came a time during that first year when I realized that Carl and I were never, literally, never alone with each other anymore. Always, there was someone present, always there was someone who might at any moment enter the room. At times I longed most of all to be alone with him, but to give him the care he needed without that army of helpers was impossible. Besides, he seemed to want the company, the turmoil, the constant pressure of people. Sometimes I felt like crying out, the man is dying—why do we surround him with this circus? But I only stated *my* need; his was to have life, that desperate circus, swirling about him so it could reach his dimming senses and make him feel still a part of it all.

Yet, some of the nurses became very important to me, over and above the nursing services they performed for Carl. There was one in particular, who covered the midnight to 8:00 A.M. shift, a woman somewhat older than I, gray-haired, open-faced. She was a capable and well-trained nurse, also a character. She would work only long enough to earn the money she needed to quit working for at least six months. She was fond of drifting across the country, sleeping outdoors, and would hitchhike, whenever the spirit moved her, carrying her belongings in her backpack, her cat in her arms.

She set out to prepare me psychologically for the last stages and the time after and she did it with gentleness and a mystical sense of the continuity of life. She described clinical death to me and never balked at answering my questions honestly. She was different in this from most of the other people I had to deal with. She seemed to understand my need for making pictures in my head in advance of the event. We spent many hours talking about the indefinable boundaries between body and psyche; we spoke about natural death and hospital death, about the way an animal dies and the ways men have devised for postponing and evading death. We spoke openly about the pros and cons of euthanasia and the practical means for carrying it through. She did not believe in it, for she believed in transmigration of souls and the transmutation of the body into various shapes and forms of existence. But she did believe passionately in the rights of the dying and more passionately in the essentials of living.

Our relationship lasted a few months, for she felt the need for travel sometime during the spring and when she did, nothing could hold her back, and so she left us. Yet the effect of our relationship was greater and longer than its duration. It was a very intense relationship. In the depth of long nights in a circle of darkness, keeping watch over a dying man, we cut through all the unessentials by which relationships are usually defined. We knew little about each other and somehow disregarded much of what we did not need to know. I gave her something, too, for she said she had rarely found anyone as receptive as I was to her attitude toward the death experience. She was the only person, during those months, who "left" without my feeling anger or deprivation. I felt gratitude for this on-the-road encounter with a well-traveled, seasoned woman of considerable wisdom.

Another of the nurses important to me was Beth, who took her place and stayed almost to the end. Of all the nurses on the case she was the most scientific, the most intellectual. She performed, in a number of ways, the responsibilities a family physician might have performed in the last months of illness, if such a thing as a family physician who attends the dying in their homes were still available in this country. She advised me and the other nurses on the handling of various complications; she anticipated emergencies and prepared us for handling them. She taught me how to beat the hospital system to get what I needed. She was tough-minded, complicated and reserved and the fine thing that happened was that she gave up some of her reserve to me.

We nearly became friends, but somehow the friendship could not transcend the duration of the event. This is something I can say without regret and in deep appreciation.

And then there were miracles, the mysterious confluence of need and response, the coming together of people out of nowhere to walk beside you when they were most needed. Chief among those "miraculous" events was the appearance of Jane in our lives.

An energetic, youthful-looking black woman, who is the mother of four and the grandmother of two, Jane had been our part-time housekeeper several years earlier. Born and raised in the South, she had had only scanty schooling and this fact made her career choice, nursing, an impossible aspiration. Family responsibilities and the need to earn a living had kept her from earning a high-school diploma, although she intermittently went to evening school to prepare for the equivalency test. After a few years of working for us, she had left in order to take a job as a hospital aide, which would allow her to work her way up to a degree in practical nursing. To become a licensed practical nurse seemed to her, by then, to come as close to her initial goal as was realistically possible at her age. We had met a few times over the next years. Jane was happy working at the hospital and still struggling to attend night school and prepare for her high-school test. I could only admire her tenacity and drive.

A few weeks after Carl returned from his first stay at the hospital, I found a note in the mailbox from Jane. She had heard of Carl's illness and would like to help in any way she could. When she came to visit, she offered to help me out as a relief nurse whenever I might need her. "I haven't got a degree," she said, "but I work with long-term cases at the hospital and I do all the work the practical nurses do."

As if I were worried about her competence . . . I was concerned with her taking on more than she could handle.

It was no great problem for her, Jane insisted. She was on the late night shift at the hospital and she had "double-shifted" before. Besides, she would only do it until I could find a permanent nurse.

Just then, her offer was too good to refuse. I had been trying for weeks to find someone for the late afternoon–early evening hours, a four-hour shift, but it had proven difficult. It was characteristic of Jane that I had to argue with her to let me pay her for her work. She finally agreed, which made it possible for me to accept her generous help which, I understood, came out of friendship. I did not know then, nor did she tell me until much later, that in order to do what she did, she had, at least for a time, given up the schooling that meant so much to her.

So Jane came part time and stayed, without further discussion, to the end. She was with us through some of the very worst hours and she was with us the last day and after. She worked afternoons for a time, Sunday and vacation relief, whenever I could find no one else, and full time for many weeks and months. During those periods she worked sixteen hours a day at nursing, slept when her patient slept and for a few hours at home. She did what a sister or mother might have done and what no one really has the right to expect of another: she made a full commitment.

Despite her lack of formal training, Jane was a superb nurse, skillful, resourceful and caring. Carl trusted her as he trusted only me and our children. He confided his fears and his feelings to Jane as he did to none of us. Her very presence seemed to calm him. Stephanie and Danny relied on her as they relied only on their closest friends. In the months when we needed three shifts of nurses each day (six nurses on staff and one for relief), she brought some of her co-workers from the hospital, each carefully selected by her. The way Jane took us on when she did somehow offered a kind of hope in miracles—that at the worst time help of a kind most needed would somehow appear. Without our ever speaking about it, Jane helped me to learn to accept help. Dependency is terrible only for those who live in the illusion of self-sufficiency and independence. We all need help at times, help of a kind neither money nor barter of services can repay. The only payment possible is to become the kind of person who can give such help to others. Jane was not the first to set me such an example; my uncle and aunt, the Muellers, had earlier shown me the way, but I had not understood it then.

Dependence on others can be an act of grace, an acceptance of our common human weakness. Acceptance of help without false pride is the last gift the dying can make the living. It is a handshake, a handhold, celebrating our mortality and our transcendence of it through kindness.

1934–1968

More and more it became evident that the past must be retraced in order to survive the present. The pieces must be joined together with patient, often blind fingers out of the memories, the ashes of destruction, the suddenly revealed meanings.

At the center of my experience with death stands the figure of a gentle, scholarly man, my uncle, Dr. Alexander Mueller. His fate and that of his wife Klari have touched my life in many different ways, sometimes in actuality, sometimes in the myth I have spun about them.

All those close to him called him "Mueller," a name as commonplace in German as "Smith" in English. He never used his first name. He grew up in a small Hungarian town, where Jewish families lived the life of outsiders, secure only in the closeness and warm religiosity of the family circle. He studied medicine in Vienna, served in the Austrian Army during World War I, was captured on the Russian front and imprisoned in Siberia for four years. He was nineteen years old in 1916; the long years as a prisoner of war shaped his life decisively.

The town in which Mueller was born changed countries as the result of the Versailles Treaty, part of the vast redrawing of the map of Europe. The town's inhabitants voted on their respective citizenship during a plebiscite, but the prisoner of war, unaware of the event, missed his chance. When he returned in 1920 neither country would accept him as a citizen. Equipped with a shining new Nansen passport issued by the League of Nations, he became officially a "stateless person." He completed his medical studies in Vienna, undertook the study of psychiatry under Alfred Adler, the founder of Individual Psychology. When he married my mother's youngest sister, Klari, she too became a stateless person, losing her citizenship through marriage.

In the early 1930s the couple settled in Berlin, where Mueller established a practice, led a counseling service, taught at the university and helped to promote Individual Psychology as a teacher and therapist. His career was abruptly cut short by the Nazi accession to power. German Jews enjoyed a period of respite, despite some hardships, but stateless persons became outcasts at once. Long before the general holocaust, Mueller and his wife began their long years of refugee existence.

It was during this period that they first touched my life peripherally. Until then they had been for me no more than names in the family kinship network. Poor Aunt Klari, crippled since birth with an "open hip," almost dwarfed, walking with a strange swinging motion of her weak leg. I remember staring at her childhood photographs, trying to imagine what it must be like being crippled. Such a sweet and gentle face . . . I thought of the man who married her as a somewhat romantic figure, a man who would choose a crippled wife above all others. I was thirteen when I first met them at our home.

They were quite different from the couple of my imagination: he was slight in stature; his freckled face seemed unhealthy, unmistakably a bookworm, a coffee-house dweller. Olive-skinned, dark-haired Klari seemed unprepossessing to me, especially compared to my elegant mother. They were the first refugees I had ever met; they were poor; all they owned were the few possessions in their suitcases. I was surprised that despite their tragic condition they could act so much like ordinary people, that they could laugh and joke and tell long anecdotes of their Hungarian childhood. I remember only one scene clearly from their visit: one morning, quite late, I knocked at the door of my father's study, which they were using as a guest room, to ask if they wanted to come for breakfast. They called me in and I found them in bed together, dressed in pajamas and reading a newspaper. Instead of asking my question, I ran out in extreme embarrassment. I had never before seen a man and a woman in the same bed. My mother and father had separate rooms and in all my childhood I never saw them kiss or even embrace. I knew the facts of life from medical books my father had shown me and my head was stuffed with literary descriptions of great romances, passionate trysts, desperate longings and tragic partings. The two aspects of knowledge had no connection whatsoever. I knew about lovers and mistresses through literature, but I had missed the casual ordinariness of a man and a woman reading a newspaper in bed together. When I glimpsed it for the first time I was disturbed and shocked. I never understood what the scene meant to me until now, when I am tracing backward, trying to reconstruct the memories of the dead into some ordering pattern by which my own life might be resurrected.

Muellers left our home very soon after this. For several months they were caught in a ghoulish international shuttle game. In those years, no European country would open its borders to Jewish refugees and none would grant any but short-term visitors' permits to stateless persons. Muellers were several times arrested for illegal entry into one or another of the West European countries. They would then be released with a deportation order and escorted to the nearest frontier by an armed guard. There, denied admission, they would be kept at the frontier post. At night, one of the guards would escort them up the line, showing them an unguarded crossing point, presumably as an act of kindness. Sometimes they walked directly into the hands of the frontier guard of the neighboring country; at other times they managed to hide out for a few weeks before being discovered. Then the process began again. Always, there was the prospect that the next time they might be escorted in this manner across the German frontier and to certain death. Finally, through the efforts of some colleagues, Mueller secured a teaching appointment in Holland and with it the lifesaving residence permit. Temporarily, they were again settled. As I heard it told, they began to build a new life and Mueller worked successfully as an analyst and a university lecturer.

During these years Muellers dropped out of my life. My growing up proceeded very rapidly and in a crooked fashion. Becoming politically active in the student underground, I jumped into experience with both feet, almost drowning in the process. Then Muellers touched me again, peripherally, through an unsettling story told about them by my grandmother. The story was that Mueller was having a love affair with a woman psychiatrist, a refugee then practicing in Holland. My grandmother, who was father's mother, used the story as yet another weapon in her continuous warfare with my mother to point up the general decadence and corruption prevalent in my mother's family. That Mueller was a relative only by marriage made little difference to my grandmother's interpretation. Caught up in the family warfare and fiercely partisan on my mother's side, I found it easy to dismiss the story as a despicable lie.

Yet years later, during one of my last visits with Klari, the story popped into my head. Klari and I were talking about our marriages, the fact, which was part of our feeling of closeness toward each other, that we had both "made" these relationships by working at them and that we treasured them as a living accomplishment. This emboldened me to bring up the old story and ask whether it was true. If it was, how had she managed to deal so well with it? I really was hoping for a denial, a final nailing of the lie. But no such thing happened. Klari was thoughtful for a moment, then said very quietly and with finality: "I have never felt deprived or diminished. If it was true, I lost nothing by it." And that was all she would say about it.

With the outbreak of World War II and the invasion

of Holland, the short years of peaceful existence ended. Mueller and Klari shared the fate of all Jews under Nazi occupation, only for them it was the second round. For a time, it seemed that by a twist of fate a technicality would save them. The Hungarian government was Hitler's Axis partner, thus Hungarian Jews were left under its jurisdiction. Mueller was able to use his claim to Hungarian citizenship, and late in 1942 he and Klari voluntarily joined a transport to Budapest, where, temporarily at least, Jews were able to survive. Behind them in Amsterdam they left the person dearest and closest to them, my mother's other sister, Manci, who was a medical doctor. Manci had earlier managed to flee Nazi-occupied Vienna by entering a fictitious marriage with a Dutchman. Now, as a Dutch citizen, she could not leave Holland. She would soon be caught in the dragnet and perish. Muellers trembled for her all through their own years of suffering and never found out what had become of her until the war was over.

I was safely across the ocean by then and spent the war years trying and failing to get my mother out of Europe. Muellers and Manci were ghostly figures crying out to me from letters and Red Cross cables, but they were out of my reach and there was nothing I could do for them. The story of what happened to them came to me in bits and pieces, much of it years later, but my feelings focused on them, making of them more than real persons. They seemed to me to be the personification of the six million others whom I did not know, who were not tied to me directly by blood or kinship. These three were me, my substitutes, my blood victims.

Muellers spent over a year in Budapest before they were caught in the "final solution." Klari was briefly lodged in a local jail, which was mercifully inefficient. Somehow, she was released and not sent off to the death camps. I could never understand her survival as anything but a miracle. Persons with much slighter physical handicaps than hers were routinely selected for deportation and extermination all over Europe, but she, diminutive, gentle, yet sturdy, survived. Mueller was one of the victims of Eichmann's death march. Caught in a street roundup he and twenty-seven thousand other prisoners were forced to march to Vienna in the depths of winter, a hundred-mile trip at the end of which Herr Eichmann expected to exchange them for several thousand trucks. Mueller escaped from the march, walked back on his own, somehow managed to return to Budapest and find Klari. Then came months of hiding out in somebody's cellar. I never found out how they survived that period; later, they never spoke of it at all.

In 1945 Budapest came under siege by the Russians. The city became a battlefield. Muellers sat in the cellar of the building, waiting for death which was certain to come one way or the other. Shooting, bombs, or, more slowly, starvation. Klari later told me about this in the flat, matter-of-fact way in which survivors speak about horrors. At first there were some potatoes, then beans. Then there was no heat nor water for cooking and they chewed on the dry beans. Finally, there was nothing to eat at all.

This they survived. They also survived the looting, raping and pillaging of the conquering Russian troops. Mueller told an anecdote of this period. Russian soldiers had liberated a grocery store and, in a mood of generosity, invited the starving survivors to help themselves to whatever there was. Mueller refused to take part in the looting of the store, refused to take even a loaf of bread. I remember my total incomprehension when he told this story—how or why anyone in his condition would act with such rigid respect for property rights was something I could not understand. He explained that it was a matter of profound conviction, something he had learned as early as his Russian captivity. Under extreme conditions a man had to decide by what means he would choose to survive. Survival by violating one's own principles, by adopting the principles of one's captors was, in his view, worse than death. If he had to descend to the methods of gangsters and thieves in order to survive, it would be better not to survive at all. After that explanation I concluded, uncharitably, that he was attempting to be a saint. It also occurred to me that possibly his ordeal had left him too weak to act even for his own survival. It is only now that I understand he was telling me the literal truth. It is possible to care so little for life that principle can be more important than life.

They came out of it clean, in poor health, bare of their past, stateless and homeless once again—but without bitterness. After some wandering, they returned to Holland, and then finally to Zurich where Mueller was offered a teaching appointment at the university. They had lost their dearest and closest friend, my Aunt Manci, at Auschwitz. My mother had died; all their relatives had perished. They had no possessions, none of the outward symbols by which men fashion their identity. Miraculously and ironically, the other woman had, like them, survived death camps and deportation. She was ill and died a few years later.

After they settled in Zurich, Muellers began slowly to gather around them the remnants of the family, old friends, former students. This was the period of their lives when I began to know them well, when, in fact, I began to look upon them as substitute parents. They were no longer symbols to me, no longer distant—they were close and warm and beloved and all I could mourn were the years I had lost in not knowing them sooner. I only saw them for a few days at a time, perhaps four times in the course of fourteen years, since we were living on different continents and they could no longer travel. Because of German restitution money, these last years of their lives were economically comfortable. The belated granting to them of Austrian citizenship removed the insecurity of their refugee status. It seemed, for a few years at least, that all at last would be peaceful and right in their lives.

It is difficult to give a sense of their serenity, their enormous resources of kindness and generosity. One could not spend an hour with them without being infected by their love for people, for each other, their sense of humor. One always felt buoyed up in their presence and even those of us who knew their story found it almost impossible to believe that such humanity could emerge from such horror. Klari had come out of the holocaust a seriously ill woman. Arthritis and rheumatism had so worsened her crippling condition that she was in constant pain. She walked and moved with difficulty, but her vitality was enormous. She managed to cook and run her household, entertain friends and visitors and see to it that Mueller had the proper conditions for his work. She also had begun to paint, quite seriously, and with some talent.

Mueller wrote a short book and was at work on another when the next blow fell. He had cancer of the lung. One lung was surgically removed and he was beginning to recover when he developed skin cancer on a leg. This, too, was operated on and he recovered. Clearly, his time was limited.

I only began to know him during this period of his life. My visits were brief, but intense, always, so to speak, under the shadow of death. Each time I saw him—on my stopovers during European trips and once, finally, when I came to spend two weeks with him—it was under the expectation that this would be our last time together. Mueller was by then incredibly frail, his skin was white and he appeared shadowy, as though one might look right through him. He allowed himself only a brief time for visits, husbanding his strength with quiet but rigid discipline. He was a marvelous listener and would sit, gathering a sort of quietness within him. Somehow, one expected words of wisdom in reply; instead, he responded with a humorous, usually deceptively simple anecdote. Sometimes a question. He always taught, it seems to me, in a conversational style, using an inexhaustible fund of anecdotes, ancient Jewish stories, folklore and personal recollections as parables.

It was not six months after his second surgery that

Klari developed cancer of the breast. One breast was removed and within six weeks she, too, developed skin cancer which was successfully removed by radiation. The parallelism of their symptoms has always frightened me—it belongs in the realm of the inexplicable, out of reach of rational understanding. That chance could blindly arrive at such coincidences is inconceivable. When faced with such random happenings one can only start believing in the *Fates*, secret and malevolent spirits living in treetops. Or perhaps, more comprehensibly, in psychosomatic causation of illness. But cancer? Yes, apparently.

Which left unexplained the strange symbiosis of that marriage. This, in a way, was more frightening even than the sickness. For they had indeed willed their own survival against such odds as would defy the gods. They had fashioned a relationship through struggle and trial which stood in stark and abstract strength against all the perishable and despairing clutchings of contemporary marriages. To me, just because I knew the darker side of their relationship, the triumph of their old age appeared luminously beautiful. It also had very personal and complex meaning.

They were after all my chosen parents. My own parents had failed me in so many ways that I had rescued myself only through my work and by remaking myself through my marriage. These two, blood kin and chosen relations, had similarly fashioned a work of their marriage. The end of their life seemed like a sort of preview to me, perhaps a model to which I ought to aspire.

Certainly, I'm hooked into their death, their manner of meeting death. Alfred Adler has defined the three great tasks of man as love, community with his fellowman and work. Mueller added to these a fourth task: to die properly. We spoke about this repeatedly. He had, during the last years of his life, undergone a deep intellectual crisis. In evaluating his own life experience and the continuous triumph of evil throughout the world, he had lost his implicit faith in his own craft. He no longer believed himself capable as a psychiatrist of helping others. He mistrusted the use of Individual Psychology as a tool for healing and retraining. He now felt that psychiatric knowledge had to be connected integrally with philosophy which, in his view, was based on deeply felt religious concepts. This intellectual shift had a paralyzing effect on his ability to write. He was at work on a book which was to express his newly won convictions, but the work proceeded badly. I encouraged him as best as I could to continue with what I was certain would be significant work, but he was strangely vague and dispirited about it and made me feel, somehow, clumsy in stressing the point. Now, I think I understand. He was, at that time, no longer able to concern himself with the writing of books, the creation of theory. He was then already engaged in a decisive and agonizing battle with death. Nothing else could possibly have mattered to him then; nothing else could possibly have demanded his attention.

Actually, he said it to me, but I refused to hear it. He said, Klari and I are both dying of cancer. (He never regarded the coincidence of their symptoms with any astonishment.) The question is, he said, which one of us will die first. He spoke very quietly, without sentimentality. "She will not be able to die alone," he said. "I am better prepared." And then he went on to some abstractions about the need for proper psychological preparation for death.

I remember feeling very shaken. Nobody had ever spoken to me this frankly about his own death. I was shocked by the way he seemed to regard it as a philosophical problem. I think I mumbled something optimistic and inane about the statistical outlook for lung cancer patients. He just waved this aside and said very simply, I think I can hold out for her sake. She needs me.

That time I think I understood and promised to take care of Klari in case he couldn't. It was a farfetched promise to make and I wondered as I made it how I would keep it, but I know I really meant to keep it. He believed me and I realized that was what the conversation had been all about. Later, the last time I saw him, he spoke about the need for detachment. I found this concept difficult to accept. Like Klari, like my mother, I constantly bubbled over with vitality, quick enthusiasm, ready extroversion. Mueller, frail as a ghost, preached detachment and withdrawal. Focus on what is essential, he said. Don't thrash around. Save your energy, so you can give of it to others. Don't worry so much, don't fret and anticipate. I listened and had irreverent thoughts about the small platitudes of my guru's preachings. He was a sort of hero to me, a wise and proven man who was dying. I really wanted to accept his wisdom, but when he gave it I could not understand it. Detachment . . . I was plunged into life, fastened with hooks, greedily clutching at sensations, commitments, need. What did I know of detachment? . . .

Mueller simply sent me out of the room. It was enough for today, he said; he was tired. I remember raging about it inside myself. Where did he get off doing a thing like that when I had traveled thousands of miles to visit him, wanting to learn from him and to "give" to him? I did not understand he was much past giving and taking. He had other business to attend to than me.

With Klari I had difficulties of a different sort. She was soft, cried readily and wanted simple physical closeness. I found her language sentimental. Her expressions of warmth seemed overly demanding to me; the nature of her strength and courage eluded me entirely. Knowing full well how bad things were with her I wasted several days of my two weeks' stay arguing with her over some idiocy. Perhaps I was taking out on her my resentment at what I perceived as a rebuff from Mueller. Perhaps I was beginning my own clumsy attempts at gaining detachment. I remember I kept making cheerful speeches to her about the advantages of taking regular exercise, sitting on the balcony if walking was too difficult—fresh air, in short, diverting interests. Only later, after having lived with death for so long, did I become aware of the extent of my obtuseness. It is to both of their credit that they engaged with me at all. I have sent people packing, these past months, for much less cause.

What these two people were really doing was trying to find a way of helping each other to die. They accepted that they needed each other for it and that Klari's need was greater. But I sense that, should it have turned out otherwise, she would have managed alone quite as well as he did. She had more closeness to people; he had more strength for withdrawal. Death can be faced either way. What was so fine about them was that they respected each other's differences to the last. It would have been a beautiful gift of the gods to them if I could have understood then and let them know that I understood. I could not and I did not and that simply has to be added to the bundle of sins of omission. So, instead, they prepared me for the death that was lying in wait for me all that time. They knew and I did not.

I spoke to their doctor, a silver-haired, kind woman, who loved them both and suffered with them. She thought Mueller would have to go first; his sickness was far more advanced. It was astonishing to her that he was still alive. She promised to take care of Klari, to keep me informed. A good dear friend of both of them, a former patient of Mueller's, did the same. It was all set when I left.

On the day of my departure Klari baked a wonderful cake made of nothing but ground almonds and egg whites and lots of tender loving care. First we had goulash, heavy, with grease eyes and dumplings and delicious fragrance. We sat in their tiny kitchen and discussed the merits of the tilting bedside table I had bought for them as a farewell present and the difficulty of obtaining good red paprika anywhere but in Budapest. We also talked about my children, about Carl, about marriage in general. We talked about my work, about religion and about our differences of opinion, which we defined precisely and then dismissed as irrelevant. We talked about a remarkable eighty-year-old blind woman, a writer and poet, to whom Klari was reading each week. We talked about America, as though it were Mars, a remote, unreachable place. Finally, Mueller said brusquely, "I've got to go to sleep now. You'd better leave, don't tire Klari." And would not leave the room until he had made sure I departed with a minimum of fuss. With no more of a kiss and a hug than would be appropriate for a visit which would resume the next morning. Only this one was forever. Mueller's lesson in detachment.

I have often thought of the elegance of that parting, the exquisite discretion of his discipline. "Go," he said, "you'll miss your bus." Go, he meant, we will die by ourselves and you cannot help us. You are young and alive and your current task is living your life, therefore do not tarry with us who must die. I heard him very well that last time. When my time came to part from Carl I was capable of the same kind of withdrawal. Allowing him to spend his small remnant of energy where he needed most to spend it. Helping him to withdraw, bit by bit, the way Mueller had taught me.

I left Zurich and went home and Klari died four months later. I was told that during her last weeks in the hospital she did what she had always done, relate to the people near her in her unselfish way, so that they would be changed and touched with a sort of awe and sudden perception of pure goodness. She consoled the young intern who wept when he saw her deplorable X rays, knowing nothing of her past and recognizing only the sad state of her body. She consoled the nurses and found a kind word for the orderlies and a smile for visitors, even though, for a long time, she was in excruciating pain.

As he had promised himself, Mueller stayed with her. He sent me a telegram when it was all over: "Yesterday we carried Klari to her grave. She died peacefully." After that, I wrote to him weekly and never received a reply. As it happened, Carl and I were passing through

Europe on our way to India a few months after Klari's death. We made a stop in Zurich, especially to see him. I had advised him of this and called on my arrival. He answered the phone and said, very politely and very remotely, that he really did not think he could see me. It would be too taxing for him. He wished us a good journey and that was that.

At the time I found it difficult to accept that he meant his refusal, but it is all quite clear to me now. He had kept himself alive against the knowledge of doctors, against the laws of nature, against his own body. He had kept himself alive because the woman who had been his stability and his anchor, this woman with whom for thirty years he had been fighting death, needed his hand in hers in order to die in peace. So he made it. Then, at last, he could let go. He died on June 29, 1968. I am certain he went gladly. It was long past his time.

Later, when it was all over and I had had my turn at death, I asked myself what all of this meant to me. Taken all together, I spent perhaps ten days of my life with Mueller, calling a day what was only a few hours of that day, for I never saw him for more than two hours at a time. He was an extraordinary man, but such brief contact with even an exceptional man cannot account for so meaningful and disturbing an impact as he had on me. Perhaps it was the emotion-laden nature of our brief encounters that mattered. Or perhaps it was not only the man, but the legend that influenced me.

Klari and Mueller taught me what my parents should have taught me but did not, about the love of a man and a woman, about the potential of such love, its complexity and its simplicity. Later, they taught me about the force of goodness, in a way no one has before or since. I have known braver men than Mueller, but never one of such compelling peacefulness. To have come out of hell as the two of them did, humanly intact and capable of giving and sharing, seems to me to be a kind of saintliness. With Klari it came naturally, instinctively, possibly as an adjustment to her crippled body and her transcendence of it. But Mueller was an intellectual; he had other choices; he had his work; he had theory; and yet he chose to make of his life his greatest work of art. He did it gracefully and with humility. He smiled so easily; a corner of his eyes was always flickering with humor and his jokes came from way inside; even further back than that, they came from way behind him, out of the folk, the long and painful tradition.

It was Mueller who taught me about meeting death and accepting it. What he did, I have lived through. I saw Carl postponing his own death in the face of all rational certainties, out of psychic need, out of commitment to the living. In all those terrible months Mueller's example stood before me as the only guideline I had.

"She will not be able to die alone," he had said simply. "I am better prepared." It is not something one can understand until it is real. But I understand now what it means to carry love to that place. It is easier to die first and don't I know it. There are all kinds of ties in one's life, all kinds of friendships, loves, complexities, but there is only one person whom one needs for dying. To have such a person is a great good fortune. To be that person, to have been such a person, is a heavy and blessed experience. *You Shall Be a Blessing* is the title of the only book Mueller finished during his lifetime. It seemed an embarrassingly sentimental title to me at the time I first saw it. Now it seems simply wise and true. Once at least, in each lifetime, we are meant to be a blessing to another. There is nothing more to know than that. The rest is just blindly submitting and bearing whatever life dishes out to us. Mueller showed me that that is not enough.

September 1972–
January 12, 1973

The summer you died, love,
inch by inch, we searched
the past for treasure,
pirate's loot: the glimpse of
an eye, quick wit, the old voice.

Cheshire cat smile hovering
over the bonehead.   Monster, what
have you done to my love,
deserter?   You are leaving
me.   You have left.

Old age in four months.   Tottering
grin pasted over your face.
Only the eyes left, naked before
what is coming, what must come—

Who stood on the precipice,
stared hard into the abyss,
demanded the next ten minutes,
then more and more.   Sheer nerve

when pale horses are stamping
impatience, mouths spewing foam,
gates creaking close into
the fog and only a string,

thin string holding back the sun—
Why wait, my love, why delay?

Into the roar of the sea
let go
let it pass

    Each day survived without falling back is a
triumph. Each day survived is a gift, a treasure.
  How small our world has become, how shrunken. You

struggle for each step, love. Your daily toil of muscle-moving as monumental and heroic as the dashing adventures of Alexander, conquering worlds. You are conquering lapsed circuits in your brain, breaching severed connections, recreating functions where they have already ceased. The effort is exhausting. You sleep each night as though you were dead—serene, remote, cold. I'm frightened by the gravity of your sleeping features and avert my eyes.

Yet each day brings joy. We touch like children, speaking with fingertips. You offer your body to be stroked and cared for as a child offers his, quite naturally, without shame, only for the pleasure of it. You seek the small pleasures, like hoarding pebbles.

No promise, no hope. For me it's floating in water on my back, supporting myself by the air inside me, holding up all that weight by making myself hollow. . . .

I shall sink later. I shall go under the water to the bottom where the snakes lie, where the seaweed grows. I shall vanish in slimy tangles of lake bottom mud. Meanwhile, I offer you pebbles, smooth, hard stones. Comfort—at long last nothing but comfort.

In writing about our complex relationship with nurses and helpers, I have anticipated events which actually occurred later. In the fall of the first year we still lived in some approximation of normalcy. We had only the day nurse and Jane, several days a week, for a part-time shift. Carl took his daily walk outdoors; friends and students came to visit; once in a while we visited friends for an evening. We even went to the movies. These excursions took a lot of planning and maneuvering. We carried all kinds of supplies—water, his medicines, a sweater, an inflatable pillow—anticipating every possible contingency. We planned how many steps he would have to take from the car to wherever we were going; we worried about getting him through crowds; we provided rest stops and quiet corners for recuperation. Sharon was great at this; she took no end of trouble to make such excursions possible. We made a joke of our complex preparations and quickly learned that there was an advantage to being visible as accompanying a patient. Carl, always neatly groomed and wearing a dashing hat to cover his baldness, looked least conspicuous of the three of us. Sharon wore her uniform on outings, although she usually worked in jeans indoors. I was the carrier of our assorted junk and, usually, the driver. After a while we got so we claimed the privileges of infirmity with jaunty self-assurance, and felt triumphant over each obstacle we conquered. Carl's elation over these outings made it all worthwhile.

A number of times he had seizures when we were away from home. I kept worrying over that and once discussed it with him. Was it right to try and do all these things as though to deny his condition? Were these expeditions too much of a strain on him? He was vehement in his denial. He would continue to get out of the house as long as he could and if it brought on a seizure, the hell with it. Very well, that's how we played it.

For it was obvious that his condition was not leveling off to a plateau. All the hopeful talk of early September, when he had even spoken of trying to work again at home, had stopped. His right arm showed no improvement; the hand was and remained paralyzed. All the exercising he did seemed at best to enable him to slow down the process of clearly perceptible deterioration. His walking was getting worse. Dr. Goldman ascribed this to a drug reaction and began a complex process of gradually shifting him from one drug to another in order to offset these "side effects." Privately, he told me that he could not really tell what was drug side effect and what was the spreading tumor. It might be one, it might be the other; it might be a combination of both. For the time being the best approach was to treat it as a drug reaction. It was his view that if we were dealing with a spread of the tumor, this would shortly manifest itself in much more dramatic symptoms. So uncertainty over the cause and frequency of seizures had to be accepted and with it uncertainty over what was happening

in Carl's brain and body. During this period we followed
an ostrich policy, trying as best we were able to ignore
the whole thing.

Whatever the reason, Carl had trouble keeping his
balance. He wobbled as he walked and had to be supported firmly when walking or shifting his position. He
had several falls; each time it happened when he was
trying to do something unaided. One fall, on a visit to
the doctor, was quite spectacular. I had taken him there
alone, on a rainy day, and was carrying two umbrellas,
his coat plus a shopping bag filled with the usual junk
we carried on such outings. There was no one else in
the doctor's waiting room when we arrived. It was a
place cluttered with straight-backed chairs and low tables, on which a few old magazines lay scattered. Carl
wobbled, trying to sit down, and pitched forward. I saw
it happening, was too far away to catch him, but could
see he would fall into the corner of a table, so I made a
forward tackle, knocking the table aside and falling into
his path so he could land on top of me, which he did.
Umbrellas, coats, bags and chairs went clattering in all
directions and there we were: me on the floor clutching
the leg of an overturned table; Carl on top of me; both
of us unable to rise and laughing hysterically. Several
doors flew open and doctors and nurses ran out to sort
us out and get us upright. Miraculously, no damage was
done, except psychological. Despite our making a big
joke of it, we were both pretty frightened by what it
meant and by what might have been. Drug reaction,
drug reaction, we mumbled our incantations.

He was very depressed for several days in a row and
when he was depressed, he was unable to sleep. Restless
nights, overfatigue, difficult days. It was the week before
Thanksgiving. When I came home from work one day,
I noticed his agitation even as I entered the room. He
barely waited for me to get my coat off, before he said
he wanted to speak to me. Stalling for time, I walked
into the other room. The nurse went with me and told
me he had insisted on getting all the mail and opening
it. Since the nurse normally gave him the mail ad-

dressed to him, this meant he had been going through my mail. Something in the mail had upset him. "Has he done this before," I asked, "look through the mail?" Yes, for a few days—she had not thought it unusual. But it *was* most unusual for him; in our long marriage we had always been scrupulous about respecting the privacy of the other's mail.

I did not have to wait long to find out which letter had so upset him. The mail lay, as usual, unopened on my desk, except for a letter from one of the insurance companies, which was the one he had opened. I glanced at it. It was the monthly claim form for disability insurance, which Dr. Goldman had filled out for me and which I then would forward to the company. It required the doctor to state, each month, what the diagnosis was and when he expected the patient to return to work. Dr. Goldman had filled in "Diagnosis: Malignant brain tumor"; "Return to work—indefinite." I cursed the doctor, his office nurse, the insurance company, myself. No wonder Carl was upset. Was it necessary to say "malignant"? Would not "brain tumor" have been sufficient?

I sat down by the desk, too shaky to move. This was it, I knew, the moment I had dreaded. The moment so long played out in the imagination, the moment when he would have to be told the truth. Or perhaps he already knew the truth which he had been seeking himself through his unusual action of opening my mail. Strange, though I had prepared myself a thousand times for this moment, now I had no idea what to say or do.

Carl was lying in our large bed, where he liked to take his afternoon nap. "Close the door," he said quite formally.

I did and sat down on my side of the bed, cross-legged, looking at his dark and hostile face and wondering how he would react if I touched him.

"I saw the insurance form," he said.

"Yes."

"What does it mean?"

Was he kidding? He must already know—how could

he not know after reading it? Sometimes people don't want to accept such facts, even if they are told—wasn't that what Dr. Wolbrenner had said? "You know you had a brain tumor," I said as casually as I was able.

"It didn't say 'had.' It said 'diagnosis: brain tumor.' "

The way he went about it made me think that, after all, he was not ready to "know." So I stalled for time some more. "It's just an insurance form. The nurse in Dr. Goldman's office probably copied it from his records."

"He signed it."

"Sure he signs it. That doesn't mean he reads it."

"Malignant brain tumor," he said. "You never told me it was malignant. And he said I won't get back to work."

"He said return to work indefinite. He's trying to get you disability pay," I said, tossing that ball in the air like a magician who tries to distract you with one hand while the other hand reaches in your pocket. Hand reaching into his pocket for his wallet. No, not his wallet, his life.

"That means I have cancer?" he asked cautiously. I had a sense of his having prepared these questions, making them slow and step by step, each small step a bit closer to the edge of the abyss, trying to keep control of himself, of me, of the uncontrollable monster. His careful, measured way of speaking, the voice so low and restrained and drained of emotion, made me think there still was time for evasion. After all these months of waiting for the moment when I would finally be able to share the truth with him, I now wanted nothing more than a delay, another delay.

"They removed a malignant tumor," I said, matching his caution with my own. I would answer each question honestly, as I had decided to do; no more than that.

"Why didn't you tell me?" He let the full force of his anger come at me. "We had an agreement about being honest—how could you not tell me? . . ."

"You didn't ask," I said miserably, tears coming to my

142

eyes. How utterly unfair that now I should be blamed for this.

"You lied to me. How could you do this to me?"

I didn't try to hold back the tears, those damn tears that always come to me not out of grief but out of anger. Tears over false accusations. And what difference did it make, anyway, whether he blamed me or not? I was the messenger with the evil news. "The doctors said I mustn't tell you. I wanted to all the time, everyone said it would be bad for you, you would suffer more, you'd lose hope. I decided finally, just the same, to answer every question you asked honestly. But you didn't ask."

"I trusted you," he said more softly. "Why should I have to ask?" This was the most terrible thing of all. I just cried. "You should've told me," he repeated, but not so angrily anymore.

"I very much wanted to—"

And then I had to touch him and leaned forward against his chest and he said, "Don't cry, it's all the same now." For a very brief time it seemed to me it would be all right. He would ask the next question and I would tell him and then he and I would be together again, sharing this horror as we had shared everything else. I could feel him concentrating and then he said very quietly, "Look at me. Look in my eyes," and I knew it would not go well, there was so much fear in me.

I turned my face to him, but that was not enough, so I sat away from him, trying to think of yoga deep breathing and taking control of yourself. What I saw was Carl the way he used to be, in command of himself and of me, and he said, "I want the truth now."

I nodded, and then I waited. Even the messenger sent to bring the bad news waits until he is asked. Nobody had sent me. It was just left to me.

"What are my chances?"

"Not so good," I said. "Very bad." We looked at each other and then I added, "Very, very bad," because I saw in his eyes that he was bracing himself for that and then politely, almost formally, I repeated what the doctors liked to say: "But you know, that's based on statistics and it's meaningless, because it depends which side of the statistics you're on."

He waved this away with the hand that could move, impatient at the irrelevancy of it, and then I had to look away from him at the blanket in front of me. They teach you all kinds of things in life, how to make polite conversation and how to sidestep an argument, how to lie gracefully, how to disguise an insult. Nobody teaches you how to tell the man you love he will die very soon and very horribly. Miracles happen, Dr. Ambrose had said. Perhaps he would not ask me when. Did I really know? The next time I looked at him I again saw that preparedness in his eyes and before he could ask the next question I added, "It looks just about as bad as it can look." I thought, that's all I'm required to say, nobody can expect me to say more than that.

Carl said, "You should've told me sooner," without anger now, softly, sadly.

"I wanted to—"

And that is all I remember. I have thought about that moment over and over again in these years that have passed and I cannot remember anything more. Except the questions that were not asked: Did they remove the whole tumor? Is there more malignancy? Will it hurt? And the answers that were not given. I imagine the fact I cannot remember means that I feel badly about the answers not given, the way I backed out of telling him everything all at once. Or perhaps it means that I continue to feel guilty about not having told him sooner. Perhaps I did right, after all, to respond to his reticence, perhaps it was pity that made me stop. Or cowardice— but what on earth difference does it make? I did tell him he was dying and what was there left to say after that?

As long as we look at death from the shore of the living, it seems, indeed, that such a fact—a man learns he is dying—should be final. For months I had thought that way about it: the problem was how to tell him, when to tell him. Once he knew, everything would change. I never asked myself how it would change. I had no experience to guide me. Once he knew, I had thought vaguely, we would be in this together and it would be easier. Like all the living, I was concerned with lessening my own pain.

In truth, there is no equality with the dying, no sharing. A man learns he will die and that moment separates him from the living. There is no way to bridge that. Yes, for the last time, he and I were sharing pain, but he would be dead and I would be alive and whatever that meant was what the next months were about. As I see it now, that "big moment," that "big question," was only a way-stop in the slow process of dying. That process is not over yet for me, even as these words are being written. He is dead and I am still trying to come to terms with this fact within myself so that I can survive as a living person, not a ghost. As would happen many times when there were decisive shifts from one stage to another, the "decisive moment" turned out not to have been so significant after all. Carl undoubtedly "knew" before I told him and certainly many times refused to "know" after I told him. He was already deeply caught up in the process of dying and conscious knowledge was only a minor aspect of it. Just so it is with me now: the fact of his death, his absence, is incontrovertible. I "know" it in many different ways and with many different modes of perception. Yet, to this day, I still do not "know" it the way I know other facts. It shifts; it wavers—sometimes it is as true as a rock; sometimes it is as true as a bad dream. I imagine it must be that way for the dying until that final stage when they really "know"—then they let go.

Carl seemed more relaxed the next few days and slept better. He was very gentle and loving with me, as if to show me he had forgiven me for my deception.

We had a semblance of a normal Thanksgiving dinner with friends out in our country house. Both children were there and it all went well that time, without seizures and mishaps. I had been lucky enough to find a local carpenter who, sympathizing with our problems, came over on a holiday weekend to help us plan a new staircase for both the front and back doors, designed to give Carl easier access to the house. The old stairs were sharply pitched and very high. Carl took part in the planning and in the decision to go ahead with building the new stairs, which would make it easier for him to use the country house. The children and I spoke about it outside of his hearing; we did not really expect he would be able to come out there often, but decided it was worth it even for a few times and in order to give him the pleasure of planning and supervising. His enjoyment in that had been so noticeable it had impressed us all. We also spoke to the carpenter about ways in which we might "later" convert the new staircase to a ramp for a wheelchair, which the carpenter thought was quite feasible. That was the kind of time it was: Carl, who "knew," planned an addition to the country house and I planned a ramp for the wheelchair he did not yet need and thought it a sane thing to do. Strangely, we each of us knew the absurdity of our actions and deliberately continued to act "as if," because that seemed to be the only way we knew to deal with our reality.

Something was going on. The next six weeks were a period of transition, outwardly fairly stable, but clearly something was going on inside Carl's body which none of us wanted to acknowledge. He had good days; he had bad days; we continued his normal routine, took him to the hospital for rehabilitation exercises, to the doctors for checkups, to the movies, to a restaurant once, and even to the museum. His walk was erratic: some days as it had been, some days much worse. He fatigued very easily and complained of pain in his right leg. Then a few headaches. There were some episodes of memory loss—one time he could not remember an activity of a few hours before, another time he had difficulty recognizing an object. The doctors said most of these symptoms might be temporary aftereffects of seizures, especially since the symptoms did not recur, but shifted, and

he was otherwise completely alert, intellectually sharp—
in short, his usual self. I found it difficult in my own
observation of him to distinguish an impaired function
which was clearly physical in origin from one which
might be the result of depression, fear, tension. Sharon
and I observed that his walk was very unsteady when
the weather was bad. For some days he even refused to
go out, when it was windy or cold. Sharon finally got
him to express his anxiety about the onset of winter—he
feared he might not be able to walk outside at all anymore, especially on slippery ground or against the wind.
She persuaded him to take a positive attitude, as he had
done up to now, and to try harder. With much effort,
he succeeded in walking his usual rounds of the garden
on a cold, windy day and once, under an umbrella, in
the rain. This achievement so boosted his spirits, his
walking and general physical coordination improved.
We concluded that "achievements" were more important to his well-being than anyone had thought, and
marveled at his resilience and fighting spirit.

For a few weeks there was an encouraging improvement in the mobility of his right arm and, more impres-
sively, in the hand which had not shown any improvement since the onset of the illness. The physical
therapist, who worked with him twice a week, detected
a strengthening of the grip and greater range of motion
in several finger joints. What foolish spurts of hope were
engendered by such passing phenomena. . . . For each
"advance" was soon offset by some loss, and the condition wavered and fluctuated in absurdly erratic swings.

It was during this period that I began to keep a daily
medical log in which the nurses and I entered our observations. I thought it might be helpful to the doctors,
and sometimes it was; but mostly it was helpful in trying
to see whether there were any patterns to symptoms
and to check out what might be drug reactions from
genuine symptoms. There was another function the
"log" performed for me: it helped me to keep a scientific, somewhat detached attitude toward the erratic
progress of deterioration. I forced myself to observe

with some objectivity and to deal with each symptom as it appeared. This checked my tendency to anticipate disasters. I think Carl also worked out an attitude for himself during these weeks of transition. His attitude was to fight each symptom separately as it came along, and not to give in one inch. Knowing that his illness was terminal apparently made him only more determined to make the monster fight for each advance.

What spirit the man had. . . . Some of his students arranged to have a movieola brought to our apartment, so he could view the films they brought him for criticism. Although it was very exhausting for him, he spent several evenings working with individual students and even participated in jurying student films. Though his gait became more and more unsteady and we were increasingly aware of time running out on us, he found ways of involving himself with people and participating in their lives.

He wanted to send another letter to his friends as he had done during the summer, this time instead of Christmas cards, which he felt would be inappropriate. He dictated that letter to me and we revised his draft together; he signed it laboriously with his left hand. Then he spent many days making a mailing list and even participated, with one hand, in stuffing the envelopes. The letter was quite different from the one sent in July; the ravages of the spirit were undisguised by customary courtesies. It must have been hard to receive such a letter with its demanding bitterness, its insistence on the open sharing of pain. Yet it was as close as he would ever come to sharing the knowledge of his impending death with his friends. It was his way—and mine—of trying to tell them and leave something of himself, before he changed too much.

New Year 1973

Dear Friends:

In this season for tinsel, canned cheer and plastic sentiment we have, somehow, been unable to mobilize ourselves to partake of the expected gesture of commercialized communication. Still, it is the end of 1972 and a New Year is coming. We want very much to be in touch with you out there at this time.

This has been a bad year, all around. The war is grinding on endlessly and the light at the end of the tunnel has, once again, proven illusory. Nixon is in the White House, fortified by a landslide victory. All of last year's problems are still unsolved, most of them worse than ever. It has been for us personally a hell of a year and so, for once, personal concerns take over to the extent of selfishness and we've got to let the world run its own course, without our assistance. It's been a year in which, finally, the only thing that mattered was friendship and love and concern and kindness.

There have been from so many of you such varied and rich expressions of your love and friendship . . . We want you to know how deeply meaningful this has been and how sustaining a force it is in trying times. On the other hand, there has also been fleeting concern, empty curiosity and a turning away from the sight of suffering. We ourselves have in the past, at times, reacted that way toward others, so we understand. In the speed and tension of our goal-directed lives reversal, sickness, pain and anguish are not programmed. Yet to us, from where we now stand, the only redeeming value of our experience seems to come from dealing with others on the level of true feeling, from facing one's fears and going past them. We have much joy, at times, even though things could be a lot better than they are. And we have hope, for ourselves, for you, for all of us.

We wish you health, friendship, love—
    peace—inner and outer—
      just the same and nevertheless . . .

Carl
Gerda

I went away for a few days after Christmas, while Sharon and the children took over. What I did was to attend a professional convention, trying to keep that part of life going as usual. I was cheered, in my daily telephone calls, by stories of successful excursions to the park, even a drive to the Palisades boat basin. I returned on the thirty-first and we spent a quiet, unhappy New Year's Eve together. He was obviously worse. New Year's Day he had a bad backache; in the following days he had severe difficulties with his balance. He had another fall. During his checkup, Dr. Goldman saw some suspicious symptoms and, after consultation with Dr. Ambrose, it was decided to repeat the brain scan and the whole battery of tests done prior to surgery. In order not to cause Carl unnecessary psychological strain, the tests were done on an outpatient basis. They took a week.

That second week of January was bad. Carl was in pain quite a bit; he tottered when he walked and stumbled frequently. Observing what was happening to him, he was depressed and frightened. He spoke to Stephanie about it and in his reticent way expressed himself to Dan. "There are hard times ahead," he said. Quite so. But to me, when I once attempted to lead up to the subject, he snapped sharply: "I don't want your pessimism."

As had happened so many times already, we were at different places. I lived in a state of curiously split consciousness: observing the perceptible process of deterioration, I tried to look backward or at least to experience some balance, some state of rest in the present. On the other hand, in mounting panic my mind and imagination raced ahead to the impending horrors in order to brace myself for them.

Still, the other part of my consciousness had to deal with the harsh realities I tried to evade in my diary entries; all indications pointed to a spread of the tumor. Surgery and further radiation were now out of the question. That meant the tumor would spread first to the motor center controlling the right side; after that it could turn into a number of directions. Paralysis of the right leg (hemiplegia) was inevitable, further paralysis was to be expected. Whichever way the tumor grew, impairment would be disastrous.

The medical alternatives were limited: to do what we had been doing (symptomatic treatment and seizure-suppressant drugs) or to try chemotherapy, which might at best slow down the advance of the disease for a time. The two doctors on whom I relied for guidance were of different opinions—Dr. Ambrose favored the first approach, Dr. Goldman the second. I talked to both of them at length before the test results came in and I discussed their opinions with every doctor I knew and trusted. All of which did little to lessen my perplexity.

Dr. Ambrose was opposed to chemotherapy on statistical and humanitarian grounds. There were simply not enough people who had survived long enough with a brain tumor to allow for statistical predictions. Chemotherapy was all in the range of experimentation. Dr. Ambrose could say with authority and conviction that death by brain tumor was kindly for the patient, painless and in almost all cases the patient was unaware of what was happening. "The brain protects the patient from self-knowledge."

"You mean his mind stops functioning?" I asked.

"Not exactly. Consciousness is impaired. A sort of comatose state sets in, often followed by a coma."

Was that a certain progression?

Nothing could be said with certainty about a brain tumor. "But we do know with some certainty about the side effects of chemotherapy." These side effects were inevitable and ranged from the unpleasant to the painful. Chemotherapy so weakened the whole system that, after a time, infections could invade any organ with devastating results. The patient would die not from brain tumor, but from some acute infectious disease.

Dr. Goldman, while he agreed with everything Dr. Ambrose said about the dangers of chemotherapy, pointed out that it was our only hope of retarding the progression of the tumor. Since it was an experimental process, no one could predict the possible outcome in a particular case. If side effects were too unpleasant or harmful, chemotherapy could at any time be stopped. On the other hand, it might lead to a temporary remission. His view was that every patient had a right to make this choice himself.

So what it amounted to was to select one method of dying over another, I thought bitterly. I took a certain satisfaction in stating things in that harsh, barren way— if you were living in hell you might as well forget about decorating it like a rococo salon. Hell was hell and death was death—and I did agree with Goldman about the right of patients to decide for themselves.

But what if the sickness is located in the patient's brain—at what point in its progress is he still capable of making such a decision? That was the essence of my problem. Carl and I had, as middle-aged couples are apt to do, spoken about death and our attitude toward it. We believed in life, did not believe in life after death and passionately believed in the right of each person to end his life when he wanted to do so. In order to exert this right, each person had to be told the full truth about his medical condition. Since that decisive conversation in November, Carl knew the truth. He was still lucid and quite in command of all his mental faculties; certainly he was capable of decision making. If now I shielded him from the full truth about the test results, was this not in fact the same as making a decision for him? In a few weeks or months it might be too late for him to make intelligent decisions on his own. On the other hand, if he were told the full truth and decided he had had enough, what then? I stopped there, unable to let myself think through what might follow. I was terrified that any opinion I came to might color his perception of "the truth" I would have to present to him.

That big crisis of "knowing" that had begun in April, had been acted out to some climax in November, was with us again a few months later. We were apart, even as together we whirled about helplessly in hell.

January 13, 1973

"I don't want to live as a cripple."

When is that? I thought. Hand, arm, leg—how much do you have to lose before you feel yourself a cripple? Is helplessness the measure of it? Hopelessness? Has that point been reached? And if not, who says there will not be a shifting of definitions, of energy and vitality at a later stage? And will there be speech left to inform me?

"You don't know how you'll feel if that happens." I wanted to know how he felt about it now, as clearly as he could define it. I really desperately wanted to know so I could help him, but I also did not want him to misunderstand my reaction. It would be so easy for him to think he was already a burden. . . . And he wasn't, no matter how he felt about it.

"I saw them in the ICU. I don't want that. No machines." Of course he saw them. I had hoped, stupidly, he might have been too sick to notice. But he had noticed everything and now, eight months later, he still had not forgotten the old man in the bed by the door.

"No machines," I agreed. "I can promise you that." Despite the statement of some hospital personnel, the decision to put a terminal patient on lifesaving machinery or not can be made by the patient or by the nearest family members. A patient has the legal right to refuse treatment or to refuse a specific treatment. He can check himself in or out of a hospital, disobey doctor's orders, change doctors or let the disease run its course without the intervention of doctors. The authority of the doctor expert is given to him entirely by the patient's free consent, and yet patients all too often forget their rights once they put themselves "under" medical care. The reality is that the only power the medical establishment has over the patient is the power to refuse him treatment or hospital admission in the future. That threat places a considerable burden on the family of an unconscious patient and tends to make most people treat the recommendations of medical experts as though they had the force of law. In fact, if the husband or wife or parent of an unconscious patient is willing to stand by that decision and its consequences, doctors can be found to abide by it. At the worst, the family has to be willing to take the patient out of the doctor's care or remove him from the hospital. It is a different matter once the "lifesaving" machinery has been turned on. The decision to turn it off then becomes a medical and institutional decision. The possibility of lawsuits looms, and everything becomes complicated by institutional considerations. What it takes for family members to stick to such a decision and carry it through is another matter. It was a matter of enormous concern to me in those days.

Carl and I had long ago promised each other never to use lifesaving machines. No heroic measures. I felt reassured that he could reiterate this decision now, because the doubt, whether he still felt that way, now that the situation was real, had been haunting me. I was prepared to carry out my part and had already so informed the doctors. And I very much wanted to keep him at home to the end.

When is it suicide? When is it murder? When is it mercy, when an act of grace? I lived with those questions, day and night; I was obsessed with them. Some things I had sorted out in my head and feelings: it was Carl's decision, not mine. I believed firmly in his right—anyone's right—to commit suicide, but I did not know whether I could or would help him. In either case, the children or the doctors or anyone else should not be involved in the decision nor should they have to take any of the consequences. He and I would have to handle this, as best we could.

"You will not suffer," I said. "All the doctors agree

that you won't have pain."

"What do you think I'm doing now?" he said angrily.

"I meant no physical pain."

He waved that aside. Unimportant. "I don't want to live if my mind goes."

Ah . . . and when is that? Coma? Lapses of memory and judgment? Surely, it is not going to be left to me to determine when that is?

"I understand," I whispered and hoped I did, hating what the monster was doing to us both. Love can press you into dark and heavy corners. . . . We had several such talks, spoken darkly and blindly in the rooms familiar through living, rooms in which household budgets had been discussed, vacation plans and children's schooling. Now we discussed murder and suicide and various ways and means of dying. Insanity had become a commonplace; absurdity our middle name. It was as it had been in Nazi Vienna—we talked of death as a lesser evil, of good ways of going and of bad, and freedom was defined as the right to choose how to die. I was actually grateful, tearfully grateful, for his talking to me as he did. The effort he made to let me know his wishes must have been enormous; I could feel it as his way of expressing his love, of trying, even now, to relieve me of what I had taken on as my responsibility. But everything said was also insufficient; nothing could prepare us, nothing could finally spare us.

After a time, something would happen in his face when we spoke like this, something I learned to recognize—a veil of fatigue or of withdrawal would settle over his eyes and mouth, and yet there would be a relaxed, childlike softening of the lines. Still in there struggling and yet so weary . . . I sat beside him and stroked his arm as he sank into sleep.

Long ago, staring in terror at the flickering lights and shadows on the ceiling in the children's room, it was I who could not sleep. Ghosts, robbers, death—the nameless, terrible fear clustered in the corners and there was nothing to banish it. If the child had enough courage to raise a voice for help there would be incomprehending laughter, mockery or scoldings from governess or maid. When they left, after their routine and uncaring response, it was worse than before, because now there was not even any hope of escape.

Escape was possible only on the rare evenings when my mother was at home and heard my call. She would open the door, letting the bright outside light shine in reassuringly, until the chair became a daytime chair, the wardrobe resumed its familiar aspect. Then she would sit down on the bed. "Tell me what you saw." She tried to see it for herself, the horror stuff on the ceiling, the wavering blobs, the things that went up and down with no set shape. It was the window blinds, the streetlight coming in through the slats. She explained it patiently, turning the lamp on, moving the blinds, yet finally, all explanations completed, she understood, really understood, that explanations did not matter—as soon as the light went out, the fear came back. Only her hand, her presence, could help. And she gave more than presence, she gave magic. She made it clear to the child that the scary feelings would stay, but that the child could play with that fear and tame it. "It's there and it'll stay there—it's your night show. Look on the ceiling, what is it? A lady? A bird in a tree? Watch it, now it's changing to monkeys. They're your night friends, coming to play with you."

Creativity—she knew how to teach that. Terror could be tamed by giving it form and shape. Pretend you want it there, outwit it. . . .

Now the wheel had come full turn. It was I who was sitting beside the sleeper, banishing ghosts and shadows in the corner. Doing the office of the mother. My mother . . .

She was the best of mothers when she was there, but the child could never know when she would be there nor what face she would wear when she came—absentminded, indifferent or deeply caring. Her definitions of self kept shifting. Many times, as a small child, I watched as she prepared herself for "going out," a routine of almost magical transformation. I observed the costuming, the deliberate creation of an image, the transformation of a heavy, sloppy woman into a stunning, modish stranger. "How beautiful you are, Mama," I would mutter, unnoticed except for an absentminded pat on the head. She swept out of the room and I felt discarded, together with her slip and housedress, which fell wherever she last used them. I remember fingering the things she had scattered on her dressing table: brushes with tufts of black hair in them, soiled powder puffs, open pots with mascara and rouge, feeling something bitter about her—the mess she left behind, the stranger she could become, the way she forgot me.

When she was home, during late morning and early afternoons, she wore loose, low-cut cotton dresses inside which her heavy, pendulous breasts swung free. She was often naked beneath her dress, quite at ease in her loose, heavy body. Her strong bare feet slapped against the parquet floor. She always seemed to fit herself. Centered in her own needs, she was unwilling to force her feelings or compromise.

She was impatient of little children; they barely amused her when they were "cute" and irritated her when they were noisy. I was never cute, often noisy and most of the time aggressively irritating, trying to have her pay attention to me. These strategies did not work for me. Yet my mother was nothing if not inconsistent and there were times when she was the most seductive person imaginable.

On occasion she invited me, quite formally, to share her breakfast on the sunny porch or to have coffee and cake with her in the afternoon. She did not know how to treat a child other than as an adult. Yet she played with me as no one else ever did. When she read a story, she lived it; when she took me for a walk, she would bring things into my awareness I had never noticed—

the way two colors fitted together, the way the horizon got thinner and thinner in the distance, the exact feel of a clump of earth at the root of a weed. She would teach me to rhyme and make rhythms, later to paint and look at paintings; to make verbal jokes and to invent a story world. That half hour with her was worth a week of waiting. I adored her; nobody was like her. She could be the most marvelous of mothers.

Contradiction and ambiguity marked my mother's life. She had a way of creating tensions just by brushing up against her environment, striking everything the wrong way, as though accommodation were the same thing as being wiped out. Father's mother and all of his relatives disliked her, considering her a "bad" wife and mother. My parents' marriage had, after a few passionate years, come to the point of divorce. But they did not divorce; instead—for the sake of the children and of social convention—they chose to live by a contract, keeping the same domicile and pretending to a marriage which did not exist. What made this strange arrangement all the more perplexing was that they were deeply attached to each other. Although they lived separate lives with partners of their own choosing for almost twenty years, they were each other's most trusted friend. It seems they could neither live with each other nor let go.

I have often thought of my childhood nightmares and my mother's magic solution for them. Did the same magic help her when she lay paralyzed for four years, waiting to die? She was a real artist, but it took her most of her life to find out that art was not just magic, but serious, hard concentration. All those years she wasted battling against the forms of convention, winning contracts and rights and meaningless freedom and spending her energies on everyone and everything, before she could, at last, rally herself into a tight force bent on nothing but work. . . . It happened too late and it has occurred to me just recently that it happened only after war and exile forced her away from the husband and children she could never leave of her own free will. In exile in France, during fascism and Nazi occupation and in the few months after she returned from internment camp, she painted. She concentrated the wildness and pain and confusion of her brief life into those months—perhaps all told it amounted to two years—and left a work of such promise and strength it can still move people, twenty years after her death. She was like a flare, a brilliant, exuberant light, appearing too soon in a society that could not contain her, cut off too soon, just when she had had a glimpse of the work she might have done.

After her death, when it was left to me to sort through her remaining papers and possessions—in a bare, trunk-littered room in a country house in the Swiss mountains—I found every kind of unfinished work: poems, novels, paintings, an instruction manual for artists, art criticism. That room was a storehouse of unfulfilled promise. She left a single-page note, headed "My Life," in which she neatly listed all the men with whom she had had relationships. It was another long list of blasted hopes and failures, except for the brief years at the end, in that flare-up of flowering, when she finally found the great love of her life, a fellow artist. I remember looking at that list, that terrible self-definition of a woman who always so much wanted to be a person in her own right summing up her life in terms of the men in it. The children, in the end, probably did not much matter. They were not mentioned.

I tore up that list and stacked the unfinished work in folders. Following a long habit, I took on myself the guilt of that stunted talent. I do not think I felt that way because of the many times she told me what a burden the children were in her life. Nor because she had said so often that, were it not for us, she would have walked out of her marriage. Such things are bad, but children have a secret knowledge of self-protection which enables them to absorb such insults and survive by resistance or withdrawal.

It was because I loved her and identified with her. Her desperate struggle between the demands of her talent and the constraints of society was my scenario. If she were strong enough to win, I might be free. If she were weak and flawed, I was vulnerable. I think it began during that early childhood, long before she noticed me at all, when she seemed strong and beautiful as a queen and yet there were these dark things in her. I began to defend her to others, stubbornly and childishly, and as I did, I discovered a strength in me that would grow and grow until it began to enclose me. When I was twelve, I somehow got through to her. Then, gradually, she began to take me on and then take me over and for the next six years our lives were intertwined in a strange and difficult relationship unlike any other. I was during these years, until circumstances forced us two continents and a life apart, her closest friend, as she was mine. She involved me in her life as one involves not a child, but an ally, perhaps even a lover. Our roles were reversed: she leaned on me, I protected her. Total intensity, of a kind that could ruin you for all future human relationships, an excess of love and trust, but also strength, that vital core of self-renewing energy.

It was probably inevitable that I would finally have to free myself from her. The last time I saw her, in the spring of 1939 in a tiny fishing village on the French Riviera, I was quite conscious of my conflict with her and of my need to get away from her if I wanted to survive. I knew it had to be done and she knew it, but again she did not have the strength to do what a mother should do, if it must be done. That is to say: go . . . and go free. Instead, she made me make the break and I did it badly, harshly, with unnecessary cruelty which left no room for her needs. It was, at that time, more important to me to speak the truth than to give love. Had I known what was to come, perhaps I might have done better. But I left after a fierce, angry quarrel barely patched over; I left gladly and with a sense of escaping the waters closing over me, and so, for the rest of my life, I had to deal with that last guilt on top of all the others.

I was nineteen when I left Europe, the only one of my family who had been able to secure a visa for the U.S.A. Europe was still in a sort of peace that spring and we expected that before the war broke out we would be reunited as a family and, at least, live on the same continent. So we said and so we acted, and worked as hard as we could to fight the ghastly bureaucracy for permission to exist. Possibly the others, father, mother, sister, believed it. I never did. If one wants to survive one must learn to act as if one could survive; that is the only way. I remember my passage to America, that mythical pilgrimage of the immigrant toward the land of his dreams, as six days of weeping, seasickness and fear. No matter what I tried to say and act, deep inside I was mourning. It was a tearing out, a violent uprooting, a voyage of death.

My mother's final illness was that most erratic of all diseases, multiple sclerosis, that game-playing killer, characterized as often by sudden and unexplained remissions of uncertain duration as by slow, progressive paralysis. That a woman of her vitality should be struck, of all things, by paralysis—struck first in the right hand and arm, the painting arm, and then forced to end her days, four years of such days, on her back with only her head mobile—has always seemed excessively cruel to me. . . . She dictated letters to her relatives and friends; she knew she had grandchildren and had their photos put on the ceiling where she could see them. I was told she took up the study of Russian during the last year of her life. My father—after all those years of their private warfare—mortgaged his earnings and invested his failing strength in paying for her care and her private nurse. He visited her regularly, as did my sister, and friends came often and charitably. The man she loved was safe in America and possibly the memories of the two years she had with him made a difference. She died in the fiftieth year of her life. Since then I have said this litany of consolations to myself a thousand times, but it has made no difference. For I did not get to her before she died and I did not finish what should have been settled between us. That unfinished love-judgment-guilt must have been for her like the unfinished paintings beating inside her against the immobile hands, the useless limbs, the slow rotting of juice and substance while the mind and heart stayed strong. I hope against hope that, somehow, in those last years it all came together for her, the long journey from childhood to where it ended, and that it made some sense, some pattern. She left me her unfinished work, as she left me the unsorted clutter of life in that room, and of all the burdens she put on me that was perhaps the heaviest: how to become a woman capable of love, a reliable mother and yet a person. How to focus and gather one's strength and discipline one's talent. Finally, to come to understand that the guilt for her life is not mine and that I alone cannot undo what made her life turn to flare-up and flame and the sputtering out of a great, a real talent.

In another time and place she would have been a liberated woman. In her time and place, she was flawed, unhappy and often destructive. She almost destroyed me, but she did show me what is possible. My beautiful, dark Hungarian mother . . .

End of January–
February 1973

The tests showed what we had been afraid they would show: the tumor was rapidly increasing. Danny and I went to see Dr. Goldman to talk once more about chemotherapy before I would discuss the situation with Carl. We were strongly persuaded against chemotherapy by Dr. Ambrose's arguments. As far as I was concerned, there was also a personal element involved. I did not trust Dr. Goldman to make a disinterested argument in this matter. I had learned that he was involved in chemotherapy research and that he was working under a large grant. There was no doubt in my mind as to his medical ethics or scientific integrity, but up to then I had seen little evidence that he considered his patients as individual human beings. Might not his judgment be warped by overriding interest in the research? Once started, would Carl be able to have some control over his treatment or would he simply be a guinea pig in a scientific experiment? Such thoughts, admittedly, were neither fair nor charitable and I certainly had no grounds for my suspicions. Still, they were in my mind, and possibly they should be in the mind of anyone considering such treatment.

For once, Dr. Goldman was not pressed for time and did not allow any interruptions of our talk. He began by giving us a frank and thorough picture of the condition. In his opinion Carl would soon be paralyzed in the right leg. He did not expect him to live more than a few months. Dr. Goldman had a way of making such statements in a perfectly neutral tone, which I had finally learned to appreciate.

What was chemotherapy? It was an attempt to check the spread of a tumor by giving drugs which destroy cells. The theory is that cancer cells, which grow faster than healthy cells, will be destroyed first and that by careful dosage the destruction of healthy living tissue can be kept limited. But just as in the case of radiation, it was impossible to destroy only the sick tissue. Some healthy tissue would inevitably be destroyed. Usually, this destruction hits the bone marrow, where blood formation takes place. In order to control this, blood tests would have to be taken three times a week and various other tests would have to be done regularly. The treatments themselves were given once every six weeks in the form of an injection. This had to be done in the hospital and the patient was kept under close supervision for a few days to check on possible complications.

The destruction of healthy tissue in the bone marrow made the patient particularly vulnerable to infections, and any kind of minor infection could quickly reach disastrous proportions. Of course, the steroids Carl was already getting and which kept the swelling around the tumor under control had a similar effect. There was, as yet, no "good way" to handle his critical problem; there were only choices among "lesser evils."

Dr. Goldman's full and frank discussion of all the difficulties impressed me. Just what was the record of chemotherapy results? I asked.

Dr. Goldman explained that the use of chemical agents to control certain types of cancer, such as leukemia, was well established and quite successful. But brain tumors presented an altogether different problem. The program by which chemical agents were used in the control of brain cancer was only two years old. It was carried on under a government grant in ten hospitals in the United States and we were fortunate to be in such a hospital. However, Carl would not qualify for admittance in the research project, because all patients in this particular phase of the research had been started on chemotherapy immediately after surgery. Since eight months had elapsed since his surgery, that made him ineligible. However, Dr. Goldman had already taken up that matter: he could and would admit Carl on the same basis as the other patients, should he decide he wanted it, only it meant that in his case the results would not be incorporated into the general study. I liked that aspect at once—it lessened the chances he would be used as an object for research, as I had feared. I was so absorbed with that train of thought I almost missed Dr. Goldman's next words. Since brain tumor is a relatively rare disease there were only about a hundred and fifty patients nationwide who had had chemotherapy for it—fifteen in our hospital.

Fifteen . . . Now I knew what Dr. Ambrose meant when he spoke of lack of statistical evidence. . . . "And how many of them survived?—"

"Nobody survives," Dr. Goldman said quietly. "This is not a cure. Out of our fifteen at least seven had remissions. Several have resumed work. That means I can say with some confidence that almost half survived longer than they would have without chemotherapy."

I sat stunned, trying to deal with such statistics.

"Without chemotherapy each one of these patients would have died within six months to a year."

"But Carl has already survived eight months—"

"That is why I must tell you quite frankly that chemotherapy may do nothing at all for him. We simply don't know."

"Then why plague him, why prolong his suffering?" The number, fifteen, kept ringing in my head. He'll be a number sixteen, maybe a paragraph in some young doctor's report to the NIH. As if what he already has is not bad enough, we're offering him unknown poisons to play games with—

"To prolong meaningful life," Dr. Goldman said, "as long as possible. I believe a patient has the right to that choice. We must give him all the information and, fortunately, we can get him into the project. If your husband had a brain tumor, say in Denver or in San Diego, there would be nothing more we could do."

If it were me, I thought, I'd give up. Who needs this?

Maybe they are short of volunteers in that great project of theirs—

My hostility and suspicions probably showed in my face. With a subtlety unusual for him, Dr. Goldman responded to the unspoken argument. "Your husband can stop taking chemotherapy at any time and for any reason. I might add that I myself will advise stopping the drug in case it does not give the expected result or in case the side effects are severe. This will be explained to him."

"Do you think he is competent to make such a decision?" I very well knew he was, but I wanted to hear Dr. Goldman's opinion.

"Oh, absolutely. He is totally competent mentally— and a very strong and dynamic person," he added, a note of respect in his voice which surprised me.

"Will you explain all this to him?" I asked. "I will talk to him first, but I'm sure he will want to hear it from you directly."

"I would never accept a patient for chemotherapy without speaking to him first. I want to make sure he understands completely what it means."

He urged that the therapy be started as soon as possible, if it were to be started. "Whatever deterioration has already taken place is irreversible. And things seem to be moving fast now."

"What do you think?" I asked Danny outside.

"He impressed me. I was sort of surprised."

"Yes, I was too. He really believes in this research."

"And he was perfectly frank and open and honest. He is blunt, as we well know," Danny said. "But in this situation that's a good thing to be."

I nodded. Despite my earlier judgment, I had begun to have confidence in Dr. Goldman.

"I think Daddy will go for it," Danny said.

I tried to keep my mind loose and noncommittal. But I thought, I'm afraid he will, I'm terribly afraid.

The next day I mustered my courage and told Carl

what needed to be told. The tests showed a recurrence of the malignancy. No one can cure it; no one can operate on it. The weakness in the leg is one symptom of it and will get worse, if nothing is done. The only hope of arresting or slowing down the process is chemotherapy. I tried to explain it as well as I could and repeated that it was not a cure. No one could restore what he had already lost; the most we could hope for was to keep things as they were now. I talked about possible side effects and explained that it meant he would have to go to the hospital for the treatments every six weeks.

"For how long?"

"A few days, unless there are complications."

"I will do what has to be done," Carl said simply. "If it means going to the hospital I will go."

"But I want to keep you at home." I was saying something else to him that I could not say.

I think he understood. He put his hand on mine. "I have never given in to things," he said calmly and without a trace of hesitation. "You know that. I must try whatever can possibly help."

His voice was firm and his eyes were clear and peaceful; it was just as it always had been in difficult moments when he made the complex simple and put my thrashing at ease.

Pop's understanding comment, at a similar point in his life, "Fight the case . . ." came to my mind. At his deepest, Carl was simple, like his father, simple and good and caring.

"That is what you want?" I asked once more.

"Yes, that's what I want."

We had not mentioned the word death. I sensed at this moment that we might never do so. As Carl could never speak of love, but he could experience it and express it richly, so he needed now to contain his emotions in restraint and understatement. I would abide by that, if I could.

I got up and made supper and we had an ordinary, relaxed meal.

"What will life be like?" he asked as I got up to clear away the dishes. "Like this, with me creeping around?"

I understood what he meant and left unspoken. If I take the chemotherapy, if I accept living as a cripple. "Like this." And worse, I thought, darling, much worse. Then I backpedaled, shamefacedly, and mumbled something about possible remissions. Incantations, fragile spiderwebs of hope. Not to fool anyone, least of all him—just to have somethings to hang on to.

He nodded, as though I had confirmed his thoughts.

Later, as he sat in my room while I was writing letters, he made a joke. "Write a letter to God," he said.

"Yes?"

"Tell him how cruel and unfair he is." He smiled, since it was a joke.

Later, I read aloud to him—Bertrand Russell's *A Free Man's Worship*. I had selected it because of that joke. Carl listened attentively, liked some of it, but soon asked me to stop. It was too somber for him. Was he tired?

No. He wanted to listen to the French language records I had brought from the library, at his request. He sat in an armchair, earphones on his head, repeating the silly phrases aloud, as the record went on and on.

"*Comment-allez-vous?*" "*Où est le restaurant?*"

There was a beautiful, innocent smile on his face. He was happy.

THE JOKE

*Made a joke. Slowly
it surfaced, bubbling up from
deep. Eyes turned inward, he
watched ruptured circuits
being bypassed as flooding
water surrounds stones, flowing
beneath, around, in time above.
It reached the place where*

*word and impulse connect, starting
nerve, tongue, sound.   He held it
whole long before, enjoying
with inner sense its shape,
its daring.   When at length
sluggish tongue, fallen lips
fashioned words badly crafted,
his face came alive
with a grin of delight:*

*Boy,
spitting cherry pits
hard, clean and brazen,
straight into the eye
of death.*

Two days later he checked into the hospital. Before the treatment started, he and I went in for a talk with Dr. Goldman. I was very apprehensive, but Carl was calm and interested, as Dr. Goldman repeated essentially what he had told Danny and me. He left out the number, fifteen, and Carl did not ask for figures. He seemed impressed that only ten hospitals were taking part in this research and asked what they hoped to learn from it.

"Eventually, we hope to find a cure for brain tumor. For the time being we hope to accomplish what is already possible with tumors in other parts of the body, to find a way of retarding growth, to preserve function." I noticed approvingly that he avoided using the word cancer. I thought that was kind of him. "Someday, Mr. Lerner, we will find a way to cure brain tumor. I have absolutely no doubt of it." His eyes were directly on Carl and he spoke with concentrated intensity, a kind of personal passion. "Every patient who takes part in the research project, takes part in that search and contributes to it."

"I like that idea," Carl said, "but that's not why I'm doing it. I just feel I have to try whatever can be tried before I get worse. I've always been a fighter."

"I understand that."

"Then let's get started." Carl closed the subject. He held out his left hand and Dr. Goldman shook it and the thought ran through my mind that Carl had once more succeeded in impressing another man with his style, his personal imprint. From that moment on, these two men had a formal, strictly courteous relationship quite different from their earlier one. It was based on sincere mutual respect, which never wavered even in the worst of times.

Carl signed the consent form, with all its frightening clauses, without blinking an eyelash. The drug was administered and after a few days' observation, which disclosed no complications, he was allowed to return home. Dr. Goldman explained that the drug would have no effect for two weeks, which meant that there might very well be a worsening of his condition during that time. If the drug worked as it should, there should be evidence of arrest and possibly some retrogression of the disease in the third week. He wanted to be informed at once of any and all changes.

The day after he came home from the hospital, despite the infusion of hope the start of chemotherapy had given him, Carl was very weak and unable to support his weight on the right leg. He tried to get up in the afternoon and insisted on walking from his room to the living room. Sharon supported him on one side, I on the other. It took ten minutes to cover the distance. He sat in the living room for an hour, then tried the return trip to the bedroom. It was just as bad. While he was sleeping, Sharon and I discussed what to do.

There was no question we were dealing with a qualitative change. Even if the drug should start to work in two weeks, he would be unable to get out of the apartment without a wheelchair. Sharon suggested that it was essential that we also get a hospital bed. His care, once he was a hemiplegic, could not be adequately done in a regular bed. He also would find it much easier to transfer from the hospital bed to the wheelchair.

I expected to get a lot of resistance to these drastic changes, but Carl accepted them with surprising equanimity. We stressed that the wheelchair would not mean he could not walk—but it would mean that we could take him out more often and go to more places than we could as long as his leg was so "weak." We stressed that we could always return it, once the drug started working and his condition improved. Who fooled whom with such talk, it is hard to tell. Still, it seemed easier to place things in this way, even as all of us knew quite well what the realities were.

The wheelchair came the next day and we decided to take a kind of cold-turkey approach: not only get him in the wheelchair, but take him outside in it and let him face all the worst aspects of his psychological adjustment. If we waited, it might be harder for him to accept facing his neighbors and acquaintances from a wheelchair. This way, it would all happen fast, before he could brood on it.

Carl immediately liked the hospital bed, the relief of leg tension possible through raising the foot end, the comfort of sitting up in a reclining position supported by the movable bed rest. We fixed a reading light at the head of his bed, got him a movable bed table, radio, books, everything within reach of his left hand. He appreciated the increased possibilities for self-help. He was amazingly cooperative about the wheelchair, dressed carefully wearing his jauntiest cap and muffler, and proceeded to meet the neighbors with perfect composure. We took him farther than he could walk, twice around the block before taking up a post on a bench near the playground. He insisted on attempting his usual walk and took some comfort in being able to walk fifteen steps without his cane. The next day he was able to walk to the bathroom from the bedroom and for several days after he repeated that feat and added to it a walk from the bedroom to the living room and back. He also learned from the physiotherapist how to draw himself to a sitting position.

During the next three weeks his condition wavered, with an overall deterioration of the right leg. Carl kept working and exercising. When he accomplished what amounted to a victory of willpower over muscle and nerve, such as walking the length of a room unassisted, he was immensely buoyed up in spirit. "I know it doesn't mean anything," he said on one such occasion, "but it really makes me happy. I never thought I'd be able to do that again."

His spirit was infectious. All of us around him began to focus on these small victories, seeing in them signs that the drug was going to do its job—these must be signs of the coming remission. And yet, unmistakably, there were the contrary signs: he fatigued more and more easily; although he had not had a seizure in over eight weeks, the right side of his face was sagging; the right eyelid drooped. His speech was frequently slurred and unclear, as though the muscles of lips and tongue were not coordinating properly. But these signs came and went, small, wavelike movements, up and down, down and up, and imperceptibly the tide was rising.

The nights were bad. He awoke so many times during the night that I decided, once again, to sleep in his room on a couch, rather than worry over whether I heard him calling. Often, after I had taken care of his medication or other needs when he awoke, I could not fall back asleep. Then I sat in a large black reclining chair, which had been my birthday gift to him some years ago, half dozing, half awake. The room was dark but we kept a little night-light on. When I glanced at him as he slept, I was terrified. He slept, not as he normally did, curled up and with his arms thrust out, but flat on his back, the paralyzed arm and hand properly propped up, the sheet tucked neatly and smoothly around his shoulders. His cheeks had a sunken look; his nose stuck up sharply; he looked like the old man in the

ICU. This is how he will look when he is dead, I thought, and sometimes I even got up and walked over to the bed to make sure he was breathing. Was I hoping for such a death, easy, unexpected, in sleep? I remember being frightened each time he looked like that and sitting up in the chair, my old cozy robe pulled around me, staring into the corner behind the head of his bed. I was sure death was there, in that corner, a spirit actually present. You can't come now, I said. I'm watching. And then I said, Come and be easy. Seconds later, my eyes still riveted to that shadowy corner, I laughed inside me, that harsh and bitter laugh survivors know. You bastard, I thought, you're playing games with us, you coward. Go ahead and do it or get the hell out of here. . . . Then death went out—I could feel it. I got myself a drink of water, went to bed and slept. Nothing was going to happen that night.

January 14–
March 12, 1973

January 14, 1973

It is curious how quickly one can accept the
most impossible infirmities. Carl's handicaps, so numer-
ous now and almost visibly increasing each day, I find so
totally and easily acceptable that I barely notice them.
For weeks now I have walked every step behind him,
holding on to his belt and my right hand steadying his
right side when needed. I have learned to walk with the
limping roll, at an incredibly slow pace, stopping every
few steps, which is now his mode of locomotion. Every
time he has to get out of a chair, it is a struggle, a conquering not only of gravity but of paralysis, lethargy of
the body, weight and lack of balance. He does it each
time with the grace of an athlete, truly—with the same
economy of movement we just admired in the football
players during the Super Bowl game. The idea is, as in
the game, not to give an inch and never to concede de-
feat until the last whistle blows.

He does not give an inch. He shaves every day, does
all his routines meticulously, does his exercises, eats his
meals. He never whines or complains. He angers, when
things are done wrong or awkwardly or in the slightest
way in deviation from the meticulous, orderly system he
has created as his world. He refuses to indulge in my
emotions, the needs of others or the tedium of unnecessary phrases, conversations or activities. His speech has
become blunt and to the point—straight to the heart of
the matter.

February 14, 1973

It goes on and on. One has prepared for disaster, sudden crisis, every imaginable kind of spasmodic

181

convulsion. Instead—plateau. An even level of misery, growing almost imperceptibly greater each day, but seemingly bearable because it sways slightly—somewhat better here, somewhat worse there. Tomorrow, this is worse, that is better. All told, each day is slightly ever so slightly diminished. Like sand trickling out of the hourglass. Really, it does not seem as though it could ever empty. Like the tide flowing out. It moves, it ebbs, it flows, and yet recedes. Until that moment when it is truly low tide. How did it happen? When?

As some would have it: a very easy death. No pain, no sudden choking. Just slow strangling, so sly, with a silken cord and perfume wafting above, in a pleasant soft bed, with music and red-wine colors, lush, delightful, slowly strangling. Or perhaps simply shrinking. Everything getting ever so slightly smaller and duller and dimmer and slower.

Smaller: the range of interest. The range of locomotion. We no longer go to the park. Even though the wheelchair would make it easy, we no longer go anywhere except around our prison circle. To the hospital and back, once a week, to leave an offering of blood. The white count going down. The platelet count going down. Not too much. Nothing dramatic. Just drop by drop, getting smaller.

Slower: speech is slower, reaction time slower. Response slower. Steps and movement more laborious, more studied.

Duller: fewer and fewer things arouse his interest. Only the children's activities, news of film work, very selectively, news of friends. Like a silken net tightening, invisibly, the world gets smaller. Smaller.

One sees this and tries to adjust. Accept it, find a sort of balance and security in that it will be like this. Floating down a big river on a raft which constantly, imperceptibly, is shrinking.

But no—there is the sudden brilliant smile. The sharp-witted, insightful comment. The savage, greedy squeezing of a hand.

A breakthrough. A reversal. There are the "good days."
He can straighten up and walk a few steps without tot-
tering. He does his exercises magnificently. He has
achieved. In his tiny tidy corner he has measured up to
his own strict standards.

The glass dome is shattered. The net is rent. The
ebbing tide interrupted by a gust of wind.

The tightrope walker totters and almost falls. Death is
having his little joke. The silken cord of the strangler
begins to draw the net closer again—tighter, tighter.

I'm still locked into my dance with death. Surviving and dying—two halves of the circle. How did it begin?

We sat at the seder at my grandmother's house, that first April of the Nazi occupation. As usual, she presided at the head of the table, the sons on either side of her, then the women they had married, the children—of whatever age—at the foot of the table. The eldest son, Uncle Alfons, officiated. He looked different from his accustomed appearance in his dark suit and black felt hat, which he wore way back on his head. No longer the usual salesman's humor and brashness—now he mumbled and chanted the ancient words in traditional rhythm. From the kitchen came the smell of fresh chicken soup, tantalizing us as we waited through the last syllable of the Haggadah before being allowed to eat.

Beside me sat a guest, the son of a family friend. He was a young man I knew only casually and whom I did not particularly like. I have forgotten his name, but I remember that we exchanged glances as the service went on, patting our stomachs longingly, turning our noses toward the kitchen. There was one emotional moment during the service, when the phrase "this year here, the next year in Jerusalem" was taken up around the table in tearful, exultant voices. The emotion all around me made me wish for a moment that I could believe, as the others did, that there really would be a next year in Jerusalem. My young neighbor expressed such a hope—more, a certainty. He was an active Zionist; as soon as he had earned his business degree at the university, he expected to migrate to Palestine and build a Jewish homeland there. I declared myself an Austrian first, a Jew second. He called me soft-minded, an assimilationist. We had opposing viewpoints on almost every subject and argued heatedly during most of the dinner.

Two weeks later I was told he was dead. He had left home in the morning to go to classes, had been caught in one of the frequent street searches by the storm troopers and had been shipped to Dachau. A week later his parents received a postcard: "If you wish to collect the ashes of your son N.L., present this card and Reichsmark 15 at Gestapo headquarters." I can still see him before me, a tall, pasty-faced youth with reddish, curly hair. He had freckles on his nose and on the backs of his hands. One day he sat next to me arguing about the future, two weeks later an urn of ashes was all that was left of him. That is how it began.

From that time on, death was always present in my life. If someone was ten minutes late for an appointment, one suspected disaster. If there was absence, there would be death. Not *might* be, there would be—that is how it felt. People began to leave, some emigrated, some slipped illegally across the border, others just disappeared. Some were arrested, shipped east, killed. Death came not in reality, but in absence, like the death of N. "If you wish to collect the ashes . . ." Sometimes one wished only for the luxury of attending a funeral, so that death might take on some reality.

All of the older generation of my family died; their deaths came to me as a telegram, a black-rimmed announcement clipped from a European newspaper. My mother and father died in Europe and I never even went to their funeral. I was a grown woman with children when I began to be preoccupied with death. I frequently dreamt of the death of my husband, my children. I made it my business to visit friends in the hospital, to attend funerals, even those of people I only knew casually. I nursed an old dear friend for years, when others of her circle had long since grown tired of her diffidence and slow decay. Another, Vivian, a radical, an atheist, lay in a hospital ward dying of cancer. During the last weeks, when I sat daily by her side, she whimpered, "Mama, help me, oh, sweet Jesus, help me die." A casual friend, who happened to have the same birthday as I, died of a heart attack. I wept at his funeral as though I had lost a brother. I have come full circle, now that I am at last attending the dying of my own. . . .

February 23, 1973

The days pass and pass and time stands still. We are enclosed in a plastic bubble. Outside, people float by; sometimes they come into close view and wave to us. We can see them speaking, perhaps they are shouting. Most of them say the one and only thing they all know how to say—their magic formula: "Anything at all I can do for you, you just let me know." Yes, indeed. I can think of a number of things. How about coming in for a week, each night, and getting the meals on the table, the kitchen cleaned, the food stashed away? Or how about balancing the checkbook, paying the bills, writing the letters to the insurance companies? How about taking one of us out and shooting him or her, it doesn't much matter which? How about getting up for a few nights and taking care of the patient? How about—but all they want you to do is wave and thank them. Perhaps let them make their dumb, eternal phone calls. "How is Carl feeling? How are you feeling?" "Why, splendid, how else? Tip-top. Great, just fine." I'm really glad the plastic keeps them out and you can't see them too well, anyway. Otherwise I might strangle one of them, just so.

It's that they really don't want to know. They're curious; they feel guilty to be living and going to the movies and to parties and to work. Their eyes are moist and gushy with pity; they look at me as though they were passing a starving beggar child in the street. A crippled child, with running sores. They're sorry, but they'd just as soon not look at it.

Also, they'd like me to fuel their pumps. They want information, gossip, the latest tidbit. "Is it malignant? What does the doctor say? How many months?" No, darling, it's benign and his being in the wheelchair is pure psyche. You know how neurotic men are. . . . The doctors think he'll be up and about and good as new by the summer and playing tennis which he never did play anyway and— Christ, I could kill them for their awkwardness, which I remember from my past. For their clumsy indifference. For asking. For not asking.

Sometimes I talk to them from inside my bubble. They cannot see the bubble and they hear me quite clearly. I really sound as ordinary as I look. They keep telling me how well I look. A compliment. A kind of pat on the back. Some say it like an accusation. Not only do I look well, I can talk straight and to the point about their various dumb interests. I ask questions. Lord, I know how to ask questions as though I cared. It feels funny, being a bony skeleton with a death's-head and asking them questions about their work, their dropout children, their Puerto Rico vacations. They also look remarkably well. "He began to compliment and I began to grin and How-do-you-do and how-do-you-do and how-do-you-do again." Once in a while one of them looks at me for real and the tears spring to my eyes and I interrupt the conversation with some plain words like, "He's dying, you understand. He's dying." And the person will turn away and avert his eyes and find some excuse to run away. And the next one, seeing me momentarily alone, will come up and offer help, to do anything, whatever I want, just anything at all. Just let him know.

Ladies and gentlemen. I have an announcement to make. There's death among you. It chokes. It screams. It stifles and hurts. It frightens you, it makes the blood to ice. It belongs to you—what's more it will be with you, each and every one of you, by and by. Accept it, ladies and gentlemen. It is yours.

But now, for the moment, it's mine, it's ours. Ours alone inside the bubble. And they can stay outside and swim past us and wave. And feel perfectly safe, because we're holding up their own encounters, we're holding Death at bay. As long as we wrestle with him, they feel safe. How well I understand them. How I hate them, the living. . . .

He lies in bed, round and still and strangely content. I can cradle him in my arms, put one arm under his shoulders, another under his legs and feel his slack weight like that of a large baby. He purrs. His eyes stay on the surface. "I want to talk to you," he announces gravely. It turns out to be about a little rash on his thigh. He wants powder, ointment. He wants comfort and gets it. He sighs and snuggles into the soft bed. An infant.

I hold his hand, his warm and dry hand. It all began between us with my holding his hand. Thirty-two years ago. A long lifetime. His hand feels the same as it did then. I look at my baby, the empty shell, the hull of a baby, which Death so kindly has left me as a little joke. A rag doll to play with, since everything else has been taken away. I feel his hand and I try to remember how he made love to me. He was so good at it, so strong, so inventive—except that I cannot remember and feel anything whatsoever. Death made a rag doll of him and a stuffed puppet of me. There's nothing here but mechanical twitchings. The machine keeps on running, but it produces nothing, it feeds on nothing. Dry run. Leerlauf.

If I try very hard and use my mind, I can remember. Like reconstructing something memorized. The right tributaries of the Danube. The great alpine watershed. The peninsulas of Europe. How we made love in Nassau. I can see the room, the bed, smell the sandy dryness of the warm night air. I know the shape of the hibiscus and cactus outside the bungalow. I know everything except how it was. Or the straw hut in Guadeloupe. The little hotel in Zurich. The king-size bed on which I now sleep alone.

I know how his hands felt on me, but it makes no sense to try and connect it with the slack, sweet baby-body before me. It makes no sense to try and retrace his mouth or to recapture it by running my lips along his cheeks as I used to do. I'm quite sure I used to do that.

He purrs and snuggles. Cozy. I'm so glad. It seems that what's happened is I have the brain cancer, working away inside my head, eating up my past, my memories, my life. A gloppy, sticky mass spreading slowly like lava. Perhaps in the end I shall lie there, too, content and snug in my plastic bubble. Dr. Ambrose says nature respects the brain and is kind to it by numbing it first so that one does not know. But I'm watching it happening and writing it down. So nature is not kind to me. As I always suspected. I have not been on friendly terms with my nature. So there's the result of it—it spreads molasses over your past.

Choking and strangling has always seemed to me the worst of deaths. How very nice a heart attack would be.

February 27

I'm keeping house with Death. He stands behind me as I move from room to room, silently, familiarly, a comely man with piercing, deep-set eyes. Often, he is no figure at all, just a presence, very still, like an empty space behind the words, a breath before it begins, the space between inhalation and intake. Much like the old folk myths, he is an image of what I know. For the Landsknechte *he was a lord, dressed like a knight, astride a good horse. For the believers, he was a skeleton, the black-hooded monk, the cowled figure with the scythe. There is little death imagery left since science has given us the illusion of omnipotence and death has been banished to white-tiled hospital rooms and impersonal machinery.*

In the ICU they fight Death, minute by minute. Here at home he has moved in with us, a huge silent cat crouching in corners, playing his slow and sneering cat-and-mouse game. His strike paralyzes; today the arm won't move, tomorrow the leg. Then, playfully, he lets go and the weakened limb totters back to function. The cat grins in the corner. He can wait. He can wait.

I'm keeping house against Death. I banish him by meticulous neatness. Order and precision are the signs of the cross that weaken his power. He is random, disorderly, aimless. His great claw strikes out lazily, with indifference—whatever it catches must wither and freeze. But order and purpose defy him for a while. They distract his attention; he is turned to making glasses crash to the floor, plates clatter and break, destruction run rampant. He can be bribed with offerings of broken china, promises of time—just until Stephanie gets back from abroad; just until the lecture series is over; till spring perhaps, yes? Till the blossoms open? Let the next two weeks pass and then—well, we'll see, then. He will take bribes of an arm or a leg, for a time. Offer him dented fenders, near collisions at 60 per hour; fevers and night sweats. For a time he will settle for minor disasters. Three men of our acquaintance have been taken by Death in the past two weeks—this should suffice for a time. He doles out days and hours.

I'm keeping house against Death. He loathes vigor, strenuous effort, persistent defiance. Like all bullies, he can be banished by defiance. Look him straight in the eye without evasion and panic. Change the sheets every day, do the laundry three times a week, scrub floors and bathroom tiles and the endless succession of dishes, offer food and ointments and preparations. Medicines. Magic charms. He can be bribed, perhaps, or bewitched or voodooed. At the very least, it keeps me from going raving mad with the waiting. The great cat-and-mouse game consists of the ever-present danger, the paralyzing threat, the breathless waiting for that aimless, lazy paw. It can be stayed by sweeping and straightening, precision and order and knowing exactly where everything is at each moment. Objects kept in check and balance. Edges straight, corners rounded. Chairs at correct distances apart and books straight in rows. Get thee behind me, Satan.

I'm keeping house in hell. A tidy house with a strong clean broom, sweeping ashes and brimstones into neat, even piles before the hot winds scatter them again. Grand, chaotic storms of ashes and destruction swirling around me. I'm keeping a neat and tidy corner. A bed free from germs. A room free of dust and noise. A safe haven free from threats. Only the time bomb keeps ticking in my beloved's head.

My darling looks so calm. Death has scattered hot ashes in his eyes so he cannot see, except his neat corner. The hot winds have roared him into dulled near deafness. He suffers only from the stickiness of a pillow, the tight fit of a blanket. He complains of a glow of light creeping in under the door. The pillow is turned, the blanket adjusted. The door shut tight. He smiles, like an infant content in his cradle. The time bomb keeps ticking. Death sneers in the corner.

I'm still locked into my dance with Death. In the Nazi jail, a regular civil jail now stuffed to bursting, I was held in a one-person cell together with four other women. We took turns sleeping on the single cot; four could fit on the floor by lying sideways, packed head to foot like slaves in the hold of slave ships. The air was foul; the daily food ration provided one miserable meal and that, for Jewish prisoners, was cut in half. Day and night sounds of violence reverberated in the open center hall, echoing from floor to caged floor. Prisoners being dragged into the padded cell; others moaning or crying out in pain; for several nights a woman slowly going mad, repeating her nightmares in endless singsong, finally settling into a sustained, quite inhuman wailing. We listened, unable to sleep, shouting threats and curses at that woman, hating her enough to want to kill her. When they finally dragged her off, we wept with relief and humiliation at what we had become. As the weeks wore on we too lost all hope.

One day, a faint smell of smoke came into our cell, which quickly grew heavier, although as yet we felt no heat. We could not tell where it came from, since we were caged in by a solid steel door in which only a narrow slit at eye level made the corridor visible to one person at a time. We stiffened, like animals in danger. Suddenly Poldi, the bravest girl among us, lost all control. "Fire," she shrieked and threw her weight against the door. "Fire," we all took up the cry and hammered with fists and heels against floor and walls. That moment I knew I would die. In this cell, in this iron cage with these shrieking, hysterical women pressed against me, choking—

"It's nothing. Shut up." The guards came running down the corridors, flinging open the cell doors to reveal the second wall of steel bars, which permitted us to see the opposite cell block. "A rag caught fire. It's finished, it's nothing."

There really was no smoke visible. We wept, inside our cell, hugging each other, while the guards cursed and banged shut the solid doors. Poldi crouched under the little table, covering her head with her arms. Not yet. But I would die in there, one way or another. After that hour I never permitted myself to think of "outside," of freedom. A terrible calmness, a balanced waiting, settled inside me. I would die in there—that's how I pulled my time and I pulled it easy.

Survivor wisdom: by facing the worst of all fears it is easier to survive hard reality. I was eighteen then, and I thought that by learning to face my own death I had discovered courage. What I now must find, almost forty years later, is courage to survive once more.

The third week after chemotherapy had passed and there was no real sign of improvement. On the contrary, the right leg got weaker and more unreliable. Carl dragged his foot when he walked and seemed unable to support his weight on that side. Ever since he had been in the wheelchair, Jane had come for a full afternoon shift (4:00 P.M. to 10:00 P.M.) on weekdays. On Wednesday, February 28, she had just finished his night care and was about to leave, when Carl went into a focal seizure. It started on the right side of the face and mouth and soon involved the shoulder and chest. Unlike earlier seizures it did not stop after a few seconds, but increased in intensity. Jane and I were both present when it started and we immediately feared he would go into a grand mal seizure. One of us stayed with him, while the other called Dr. Goldman. We managed to give him the sedative we had been instructed to use, even as the tremor continued unabated. He was conscious and at first able to speak. We tried to calm him as the tremor continued, without letup, for four hours. . . .

Dr. Goldman called back in an amazingly short time and instructed us to give Carl massive doses of the drug at fifteen-minute intervals and to watch for swallowing difficulty and choking. If his condition stayed the same, continue the drug until the seizure stopped. If it got worse, get an ambulance and bring him into emergency. Carl was able to swallow the medicine crushed in liquid and stayed lucid and conscious throughout, even as he was unable to speak later on. Jane, without being asked, simply stayed on, and without her I would not have been able to hold out. Dr. Goldman called back about every half hour and gave us comfort and support by his availability and concern. Four hours . . .

The seizure finally stopped at 2:00 A.M. and Carl fell into a deep, drugged sleep.

"That's why they want you to leave him in the hospital," Jane said. "So you don't have to watch this."

Yes, it was terrible, worse than anything up to now. It was terrible to watch him suffering and not to be able to do anything, but I thought what it would have been like for him to have such an attack in the hospital, with no one there who loved him and cared. Who knows? . . . During those four hours I had at times hoped it would get worse—grand mal brings coma and death—and at times hoped fervently it would stop and everything would be unchanged. Wavering back and forth, swinging, flickering with the terrible twitching of his muscles in spasm. But I had been able to take care of him, anyway, I had done what could be done and now he was still here, still in his room, sleeping so heavily. . . . What if tomorrow he would not regain his speech? What if while I slept, there was another seizure?

I was so tired, I was so afraid. Jane and I took turns, in two-hour stretches, sitting up with him while the other slept.

In the morning he was conscious, he could speak, although his speech was slurred, but he could not move the right leg. He was under so much sedation that this might have been the effect of medication. Still, he had another brief seizure that day and the next. Dr. Goldman wanted him kept quiet and at rest and he should not be permitted to try and walk. This continued for several days. We began to notice increasing weakness in the left leg. Both knees buckled when he was transferred from bed to wheelchair.

The doctor's opinion was that the chemotherapy had not "taken," and what we were seeing were symptoms due to the continuing growth of the tumor. However, he wanted to continue with another round of the drug, since sometimes it took two or three doses before there was any visible effect. Besides, there was nothing to lose, the way things were going.

On March 7, six weeks after his last hospitalization, Carl was back in the hospital for chemotherapy. This time, he did not walk in; we brought him in in a wheelchair, his right side paralyzed—a hemiplegic.

March 12

*There was some inward change in his face to-
night. He sat as though listening to himself. His speech
is bad. I lean forward to hear it and—always, always—he
keeps his eyes averted.*

*It is shame. I know that shame. The nakedness, stark-
ness of suffering is shameful like lust. One must cloak it
in ordinary gestures, hide it, pretend to have sand in
one's eyes or perhaps the sniffles.*

*It is because he cannot bear what has happened to my
face that he cannot bear to look at me. We hold hands,
warmly, contentedly, like two children in a playhouse.*

*His weakness is so obvious, it takes skillfully trained
obtuseness of doctors and nurses to ignore it. They praise
his looks, as they praise my jewelry or my hairset, anything at all they can find worth praising. Just so they
won't have to look at his weakness, the slackness of
mouth, the helpless dribbling of spittle on his chin.*

*He made a joke yesterday. During lunch he choked on
his food, coughed, unable to control his swallowing. Recovered, once again. How they love him for his ability to
recover. Good show! "You know what's really the matter
with me?" he asked the nurse. "What?" "I've got tubercu-
losis!" And he's got his old twinkle. Yeah, man.*

*I'm so glad he is joking. That kind of bravery went out
with knighthood. "Does he know?" they ask. Yes, he
knows. And then what?*

*Knowledge is an ice-cold coin. You hold it in your
hand and it chills you to the bone. It does not buy you
the warmth of a drink, it does not offer you the breadth
of a bed. No dream space. It's a skeletal certainty, which
you might as well ignore. Like the truth, it is the ultimate cruelty. Imagine, knowing the extent of one's loneliness. Imagine, measuring the depth of a glacier lake.*

*Tonight, Death sat behind his eyelids. I nodded hello,
as I nod to an acquaintance. I know you; I acknowledge
your presence. Now leave us alone, will you? We sat
looking at the night, the city skyline made of light and*

movement. Incessant flow of existence, of exertion. We sat holding hands and, without words, spoke of dying. Something ancient and wise had settled in his face. Our joint images, intimate and clumsy, were reflected in the pane of glass on top of the incessant tide of city traffic.

"I'm alone a lot," I said. I did not know beforehand that I would cry. He turned his eyes upon me fully, for the first time in many days, seeing. "I know," he said. Then I cried and he averted his eyes.

I understood and was ashamed. "Time for bed," I said and grasped for the handy activity of nursing and caring.

He really knows. So, perhaps, after all these years what we can do for each other is to spare each other from words. From needless shame and from the need of statement. Somehow, our hands have always known everything there is to know. Thank you for silence.

March–May 1973

THE COMMON WISDOM

Their marriage is a good one. In our eyes
What makes a marriage good? Well, that the tether
Fray but not break, and that they stay together.
One should be watching while the other dies.

Howard Nemerov

How do you chart the incoming tide, the rhythmic pattern of wave upon wave, the slight increases in peaks
and troughs, the imperceptible advance of tide's edge?
What scale of measurement is appropriate to the wearing away of rock by drops of water, the erosion of land
by rushing brooks, the hollowing out of rock by falling
water? Each day seen by itself was an island, existing in
its own space and time, longer than any known day because it was irreplaceable. Against the dead walls of
doomed time ahead, each day was perfect within itself,
a small miracle, a gift. Each day was still, the minutes
precious in those golden moments when acceptance
brought silence and rest. Yet each day was convulsive,
torn with useless thrashing, with resistance and effort,
with frantic struggle of will against fate, will against
body, soul against nature. It seemed these months, each
longer than the one before it, were a lifetime, an eter-
nity. To this day they bulk as chains of mountains, past
which all vision is impossible. They obstruct, they im-
prison. They have blotted out the decades before them
and have made memory into a moth-eaten, unreliable
net. The nights could deny the days and hopeful,
achieving days would inevitably be followed by restless,
anxious nights. Nothing was solid, reliable or penetra-
ble; there was only shifting and waving, shimmering

199

and slithering. The only thing stable was a dull, unmoving pain, which never lessened, never flared. It had become like a poisonous gas one was forced to breathe; it formed a baseline to experience, promising only one certainty: it would get worse.

Everything was in process, in change. There is no better way to learn about process than by living beside the dying. One still holds somewhere within oneself the picture and image of what has been. What the man used to be, what the marriage used to be, what oneself used to be in a time called normal. One knows where it is going; it is something one has words for but no meaning. He will die—what is that? He will cease to be here, he will cease to be, he will cease—but that is truly unimaginable. One evokes, for comparison, memory of the dead. It is said to be like a long, an endless absence. That is what it will be afterward. But becoming so that one ceases to be? What is that like? What is a marriage after one partner has ceased to be? What is the self after the chosen half has altered so as to cease to exist? Ah, the mind falters; it draws a dark curtain and refuses to function.

But the way, the process—living through it day by day, recording it in a medical log, verifying it through conversations with friends and family and doctors, keeping a diary, trying to disengage from it somewhat by observation—does one see? I do not think that staring hard at the ocean makes it possible to see the incoming tide. One clings to seeing only the shortest range: the yesterday, the today, perhaps tomorrow morning. That way it is possible to survive almost anything. To write in the log: "right leg much stronger"; "speech improved"—and almost to believe it.

Outwardly, time divided into six-week segments, the intervals when the chemotherapy drug was given. Two weeks of stability or deterioration, as the case might be; two weeks of arrest and retrogression (will it be large enough to offset the previous four weeks?); two weeks of deterioration. At best, it was playing leapfrog on a downhill slide. For the last two weeks of the cycle there was the added tension of following the blood count. If the platelets or the white count went down too sharply, it would not be possible to administer the next dose.

I attempted to do a medical summary of that period, looking backward in order to determine what the effect of chemotherapy had been. It was equivocal, like this:

> *Second chemotherapy 3/8. Two weeks later improvement, strength in leg increases. Third week—fatigue, speech worse, psychic stress, variety of symptoms. Fourth week—bad speech deterioration, memory loss. Steroids are doubled which leads to mood elevation. Fifth week—two small seizures, some improvement in memory and speech. Vocabulary excellent. Sixth week—speech worse.*
>
> *Third chemotherapy 4/19. First week—seizure; speech reversal; second and third weeks—improvement but speech reversal continues. Fourth week—three mild seizures on successive days; from then on steady deterioration in speech and general condition until*
>
> *Fourth chemotherapy 5/31.*

For two weeks, after the second chemotherapy was administered, Carl was confined to the house and to a very quiet routine. This was done in order to avoid anything that might bring on another seizure of the disastrous proportions of the last one. This period, which we thought of as recovery from a "sickness," formed a sort of transition to his life as a hemiplegic. We learned what that meant; we learned how to live with it and we learned that it was not as bad as we had thought it would be when this seemed the worst that could happen. We exercised as before, continually working by passive and active exercises to keep all the limbs in the best possible condition and strength. Carl attempted daily to put some weight on the paralyzed leg and many times was able to stand on it, with support, for seconds and minutes. We perfected the techniques of "transfer," which are so crucial for the hemiplegic—how to get from bed to wheelchair, from wheelchair to bed and from one position to another. These are relatively simple skills the hemiplegic and those who care for him must learn. Once they are learned they greatly improve the ease of care and the range of functioning. We learned how to avoid muscle spasms and pains in the paralyzed limb; how to guard against accidents and falls; how to boost the patient's sense of competence by never doing anything for him that he can do for himself. Whole days could be "good" days for Carl, when he managed to turn himself in bed unaided or to stand on both legs for the transfer. We learned that the hemiplegic is given to greater sensitivity to heat and cold than is the person who moves by himself. We also learned to accept and take for granted the kindness and helpfulness shown by all persons who encounter a man in a wheelchair. Dependence now became something to which one could respond by cheerful acceptance of the help of others. This was a new experience for both of us, and possibly quite salutary. At times, on the other hand, such proffered help could be unintentionally cruel.

A strange woman helped me to get the wheelchair up a few steps in the park. I thanked her.

"Glad to do it," she said. "It's touching the way you take such good care of your father."

"My husband," I said and rejoiced that he had not heard her.

Another irreversible change brought on by the hemiplegia was that from that time on we lived with twenty-four-hour nursing care. The midnight to 8:00 A.M. nurse had been hired after the last long seizure. I realized I had been fortunate that Jane had been there and offered to stay; without her I could not have managed and we would have had to take Carl into the hospital as an emergency case. The night nurse made a considerable difference in my life, since I was now able to take a sleeping pill and get six and a half hours' solid sleep. When Carl became a wheelchair patient, the informal arrangement with Jane had to be changed to a regular afternoon shift, which Jane and another practical nurse shared. I now had four nurses on the payroll for the week and two relief nurses for the weekend, with the children and I sharing the other weekend shifts. Fortunately, Carl had excellent insurance coverage through his union and had taken out two private major medical contracts. This, plus the coverage he had through the medical plan at my college, did not cover all the costs of his sickness by any means; but it covered about three-fourths of it. The rest we paid out of savings. No doubt about it, decent medical and nursing care for serious illness is a luxury item in this country.

The anxiously awaited third week after chemotherapy brought no visible improvement; instead it brought new symptoms. Carl complained of headaches, inability to sleep, pain and odd sensations in the *left* leg. The first adverse "side effect" had become manifest—raw, blistery eruptions of the skin in the groin area, similar to bedsores, which defied the customary treatment and refused to heal. Carl's patience was wearing thin.

He refused to do physiotherapy; he rejected his finger exercises by insisting to one nurse that another had already done them that day. He fussed over medication and for several weeks became a "bad patient." He retreated behind sullenness, complaints and irritability. His nights were restless; he slept fitfully in small snatches or not at all. Obviously, he was going through some sort of crisis. I guessed that the anger and despair he had been holding in for so long now were finally becoming intolerable.

There was one night when two friends were visiting. Carl, who had just been wheeled in by the nurse, decided he wanted to sit on the couch near them. The nurse wheeled his chair over to make the transfer and I stepped forward to assist, as I usually did.

"Get away!" Carl shouted at me so loudly everyone jumped. A painful, embarrassed silence ensued, then the conversation resumed at a normal level. For once, I did not take his outburst personally. I could sense the depths of his despair, which was strong enough to enable him to shout when for weeks he had only been able to speak in barely audible range.

The morning after this incident he called me in for a talk. He had come to the conclusion that chemotherapy was making him worse. He had sensations in his left side which alarmed him and to which none of us was paying any attention. This had been so all along, he complained; nobody was listening to him. He wanted to see Dr. Goldman personally; he was not satisfied with my being an intermediary. And if that conversation did not prove satisfactory, he wanted another neurologist called in.

His face was dark as he came out with that long, carefully prepared list of grievances. Finally, he was allowing the anger to surface. I felt almost relieved.

"Are you sure," I asked, "you want someone else to confirm what you already know?"

Yes, he did. If necessary he would change doctors, nurses, presumably wives. I agreed we should see the doctor as soon as possible.

"And I don't want you talking to him beforehand or afterward."

"I don't have to be in the room at all," I offered.

Carl grinned. "You can be there, just keep your mouth shut." This was comfortably familiar to both of us—the way he would put up with my extrovert, interfering ways for a long time and then, when he'd had enough, just step in and stop me. The way I would take it, meekly, as though I'd been waiting for a long time to be stopped and why hadn't he done it sooner? An old, well-worn marriage. I was able to get an appointment with Dr. Goldman for that evening.

As soon as that was settled, I left for work. Carl told Sharon about our conversation. She and I had discussed his attitude earlier. We had agreed that since he was obviously under great psychic stress, she should do all she could to get him to talk. She went further in this than I had. After listening to him, she told him she thought he was looking for a new doctor only because he was giving himself false hope of a cure. Here are her notes in the log for that day:

Carl was told that because he so desperately wants to get better and he knows he can't he is now refusing medication, neglecting his exercises and the established routine. He was told point-blank he was never going to get better. He could either allow that knowledge to consume him or try and concentrate on the happiness he still has. He said he was grateful for my telling him all this and he wants the truth. Throughout what I had to say he listened with complete attention and patience. Seemed as if he was ready to hear it now. I left the room for twenty minutes and returned to find him anxious to proceed wtih the day's activities. Rest of the day went on in normal, cheerful fashion. Carl said he was exhausted and did not want to go outside, to which I agreed. He made a list of questions to ask Dr. Goldman, then took his afternoon nap.

In the early evening Jane and I took him to Dr. Goldman. Having two "helpers" when going out on trips made wheelchair transfers much easier. It also made it possible to have the nurse wheel him indoors while I parked the car and thereby keep him from having to wait in a public place or on a street corner. Jane stayed in the waiting room while he and I went in to see the doctor. I wrote down what happened in my diary:

March 27, 1973

A year ago today we were walking on the beach in Paradise Island, enjoying a perfect vacation. Carl was marvelously tanned, lean, radiantly healthy. He had not felt or looked younger in a decade.

Today, shrunken, flabby-chested and hunched forward in his wheelchair, one of his nurses wheeled him into the hospital to see one of his seven doctors. He looks twenty years older than a year ago, half-bald from radiation treatment, one side of his face slack and pulled downward from focal seizures. His right arm and leg are paralyzed, the good leg so weak he cannot stand on it. His speech is slurred and difficult to understand, his hearing worse than ever; his memory is faulty and his weariness is great. But his mind is clear and his will unbroken.

At first Carl hedged in the kind of questions he asked, but stated clearly his determination to be told the truth exactly and without equivocation. Dr. Goldman, so often brash and abrasive, rose to the occasion by giving us undivided attention. He projected scientific detachment and a fitting tone of seriousness. He has an armor of briskness which indicates to the patient and his family that sentimentality and personal involvement have no place in this room. Patients are objects to be worked on by Science, represented by himself. What is of interest about them is symptoms, conditions, objective facts. But he responded appropriately to the anxiety Carl expressed about his "symptoms" on the left side. "I cannot tell whether the symptoms you notice are due to the drugs you are taking and if so, to which drugs. Nobody has yet tried the drugs you are taking in just that combination. But I can assure you that we are not dealing with an onset of paralysis on the left side. This could only be caused by a spread of the tumor and if that were the case, if both sides of your brain were affected, we know you could not sit here and ask me intelligent questions." Patiently and as thoroughly, Dr. Goldman responded to each of Carl's questions.

Sitting in this office where I had spent so much time fighting Dr. Goldman, I looked on him with new detachment. I saw him with my writer's eyes; perhaps I needed to do this in order to detach myself from the cruelty and absurdity of this scene. I tried to picture this brilliant young doctor to myself twenty years from now, and could not. Would his humanity, the growth of his soul, keep pace with the growth of his mind and skill? He must be the pride of his parents. He must have worked terribly hard to get so far in life so quickly, to hold the place he now held. His job: eight, ten hours a day to tell people desperate news about themselves. Perhaps he was simply too young in years to perform adequately in the role of hanging judge. I wondered briefly what would happen if I broke the spell of detachment he

created in this room and made him feel *for a moment
what we felt. I gave it up at once; he would not tolerate
it and it would serve no purpose. Besides, it was hardly
my problem. I suddenly felt sorry for him, having to pronounce death sentences on men like Carl.*

*And yet, even as I struggled for detachment, I sensed
something different in Dr. Goldman that day—a passion of his own which penetrated his armor of objectivity. He seemed to hit the right tone with Carl from the
start.*

*"You are a fighter, Mr. Lerner," he said, "and I'm a
fighter. You're a pretty tough man and so am I. Do you
want me to give it to you straight?"*

*Yes, Carl did. The oddest thing about the scene was
that it had really—not in nightmare or déjà vu—occurred once before, at the time Carl had given his consent for chemotherapy. Everything had been explained to
him already. With the difference that then he was so
drugged with anticonvulsants and so weakened by his
seizure, the full impact might have been cushioned.
Now he was stone-cold sober and wide awake.*

*"A few years ago with the kind of tumor you have,
there would have been nothing, nothing anyone could
do for you. They would have told your wife you had a
few weeks or maybe months to live and then you'd have
had a tough time finding a neurosurgeon or neurologist
who would even talk to you. They'd be running from
you, sending you from one hospital to the other, because
they would feel so bad about not being able to do a thing
for you. We did a study [then followed overwhelming
statistics]. . . . According to that study as far as we
know now 90% of all cases with your kind of tumor are
dead six months after surgery. May, June, July—" he actually counted it out on his fingers— "You should have
been dead in October."*

*Carl sat quite immobile. His live hand was holding
his dead hand and both shook just a little. I did not
realize it at the time, but I jumped up out of my chair
and stood beside him. Probably I moved from an instinct
that made me also want to slug the guy, but something*

else made me hold still and let him go on and just observe.

"Then we learned to use high dosages of cobalt radiation. You had that. That extends the survival time by two months."

We both winced at the term "survival time." Some of the doublespeak of the Vietnam War flashed through my mind.

"November, December. You should have been dead by January. So you see, Mr. Lerner, you're not doing so badly." Then followed another very technical lecture on chemotherapy. Carl sat stunned and I thought with hatred that Goldman was speaking speedily, as is his habit, in his brisk, decisive staccato to a man whose brain had to labor slowly and painfully to turn the random sounds into meaning. Just like him, I thought, not to perceive that even a death sentence might not be understood if delivered too rapidly. A fat lot he cares.

Then something extraordinary happened. Dr. Goldman, talking about the chemotherapy project, began to be transformed by real feeling and passion. Grants, money, research designs became a live force. "We will conquer this thing," he said, his eyes blazing with intensity. For a moment, even in my own misery, I perceived something noble and grand in his passionate hatred of this enemy sitting inside Carl's head and destroying his life. "Perhaps not in your lifetime," he continued, and this time the words were not cruel, simply honest, "but surely not too long from now we will learn how to arrest brain cancer by chemotherapy."

Somehow, the way he put it, there was some meaning in participating in that venture, that battle, which will go on when one's own life ceases. For a moment, with all his obvious frailties, he was on the same battleground with us, not because of us or of Carl as a person, but because we shared a common enemy. As an old political fighter, Carl sensed this and warmed to it. "Okay," he said and thanked him, patting him on the arm with a feeling of real warmth.

We left. Outside in the hall, I had to stop; I was trembling. There was a beautiful radiance in Carl's eyes. He chuckled, then broke into a grin. "I should've been dead in October," he said with a kind of awe and delight. He'd fooled somebody for real.

We laughed like lunatics all the way home, trying to tell the story to Jane, trying to imitate Dr. Goldman's delivery and manner. Carl could not get over how patient he had been.

At home, I offered him the extra phenobarbital, which he was supposed to take for stress situations. "No, thanks," said he. "I refuse to become a dope addict." Wow. . . .

He slept serenely that night.

The next morning as soon as Sharon came, he joked, "Do you know you're sitting next to a man who should be dead?"

He repeated that joke several times, then related in detail and with accuracy what Dr. Goldman had said. He commented on how patiently the doctor had listened to him and how he had given him a complete technical explanation, including statistics. "I sure don't do much for his statistics."

He thought about that for a while, then added sadly, but in a factual tone: "I still haven't got the chance of a snowball in hell." Then proceeded to eat his lunch with enjoyment. The left-side complaints disappeared and were not heard of again.

The end of the third week brought no improvement, neither did the fourth. On the contrary, the platelet count dropped; the skin lesions got worse; speech deteriorated. Carl took a long time to find the right word and often could not find it. He then would use some circumlocution, like a person using a foreign language who misses the appropriate vocabulary. One evening, to pass the time, we played Chinese checkers. To my horror, he could not retain the rules for moving the pieces—crisscross and jumping, but no moving backward—with which he was of course familiar. He faked it by moving his pieces quite at random and imitating my moves. Memory was going fast. . . .

One morning, when I came to his room to say good morning, he told me he had been up for hours. "Do you have any idea why you can't sleep?" I asked.

"The robbers rob you at night," he answered.

I understood at once. He had gone to sleep at night and awakened to find his right arm paralyzed. He had gone to sleep another time to find his right leg paralyzed. Seizures, which came at the onset of sleep, had weakened his facial muscles. No wonder he was afraid to fall asleep.

"Nothing more can happen," I lied. "Or at least you won't know it," I corrected myself more truthfully.

He shrugged. "I try to sleep anyway, but sometimes it doesn't work."

Quite understandable.

CARL'S POEM

*"The robbers rob you at night." They steal
an arm. A leg. What
is left—perhaps breath, the voice. Life.
Life itself.
They come through walls. Light
will not protect you. Nor gates,
fences. Guards, nurses, dogs
are of no avail. One must be
watchful. They catch first
the unwary. They wear
masks, disguises. One must will
them to reveal their faces. Sleep
looks altogether too much
like his brother. Trick them both
or they will trick you. With violet eyes,*

March–May 1973

green skin, soundless fingers
they wait at the foot
of the bed, one brother,
the other,
till one is tired
too tired:

then they choose.

MY POEM

The robbers rob you at night.   They steal
an arm.   A leg.   Next
voice, breath, life.
Life itself.   They hide
inside bone, warm flesh,
cutting with spider threads,
diamond-sharp, evil.   Tricksters,
they work cleverly while
we are busy with daylight
doings.   Resting at night
while we stand watch they
blink their hooded eyes,
rub their knuckles, waiting.
Only laughter, hand clasp,
the hard beam of defiance
holds them off for a time, then
they start again.   Unlikely twins, they
dispute over means: knife thrust,
explosion, smothering feathers,
decay—see-sawing brothers
they argue and play.   One brother
soothes, the other kills.
Night holds them both,
burglar and shill.   Brother Sleep
be kind, hush your twin's
silent craft.   Rockabye—

211

There was so much I had to learn in those months. Not the least of it was to cut through the myths about dying, to tear the romantic notions, the lies, out of my head and my feelings. We would not be sitting in some lonely cottage by the sea, hand in hand, sharing the pain, the evening glow of slowly ebbing feelings. We would not commune with each other in some secret way, not understood by anyone else. I would not receive from him, dying, the gift of a sustaining message, the meaning of what our life together had been all about, what the randomness and folly of his dying was all about. Nothing turned out to be the way literature and myth had told me it would be. Everything was different, stronger, harsher, more demanding. I know there are simpler ways of dealing with this experience than the way we chose. I understand, with deep longing, that there is a ritual which helps people and sustains them by limiting their choices and letting them proceed by tradition. This was not possible for us; it was not our way. We had no religion and were not about to acquire it. We had strong values and strong beliefs and we held on to them. We had always tried to live authentically, in the sense in which Sartre uses the word, and that is what we were trying to do in this crisis. One reason for setting down this record is to trace the way our values helped sustain us, perhaps in the hope that others, for whom religion and ritual are also not possible solutions, might take sustenance and courage from our experience.

Fifth and sixth week. A few minor focal seizures without aftereffects. In the middle of April we drove to the house of friends, a half hour ride. Carl could sit in the garden, under blossoming trees, have dinner on a beautiful terrace. He loved it, but seemed depressed just the same. I asked him why. Did I realize that this was his first outing since Thanksgiving?

No, I didn't. But he was right. "We'll take you out more now," I promised. It meant so much to him. We began to plan another weekend in our country home. Maybe after the next round of chemotherapy.

The third round of chemotherapy was given at the hospital April 19–20. This was followed by the usual few days of quiet recuperation at home.

The daily log recounted our desperate struggle for a semblance of normal life:

April 25. [Conversation with Sharon.] We talked about Dr. Ambrose and how he had been hurt when Carl told him last time he saw him, he no longer believed in his philosophy. This had been said when Carl learned of the malignancy and blamed Dr. Ambrose for not telling him the truth earlier. I [Sharon] asked him if he would have been as happy if Dr. Ambrose had told him right after the surgery that he was never going to get better. He said he would not have been as happy and that he now understands Dr. Ambrose better. "I'm going to get worse," he said. "How much more can I suffer? I don't know if I can stand it. I'm so alive." I told him we would not let him suffer. Then he started asking question about what he should expect from now on. "I hate these half disclosures . . ."

April 28. Motor seizure in inner part of right jaw, invisible from the outside, lasting perhaps 5 minutes. He felt it clearly localized. Dinner in bed, quiet evening, generally slow reactions. Several times during the day and on previous days changed cause-and-effect words. "Dr. Goldman is my patient."

April 29. Carl planned a birthday party for me! He and Stephanie went outdoors to buy a birthday cake at the bakery, which he himself selected. Danny had bought the gift—a yogurt maker—which was Carl's idea some time before and that afternoon (a day earlier because it fitted better with the children's schedule), we had the kind of party we always had on birthdays. In the living room, everyone watching while I opened the gifts; then we had the traditional birthday dinner, all four of us together. He was so pleased at my surprise (that he remembered, that he had planned it himself); he spoke about it for days afterwards. I kept thinking, the last

*time, and choking it down. Danny took a series of fine pic-
tures of all of us and mostly of Carl. We look happy on those
pictures, smiling and close to each other. That's how it must
have been, since the pictures say so.*

*May 4–6. Steffie, Danny, Carl, Sharon and I took a
weekend in our country house. Everything went beautifully.
We gave him a ride around the town and to the beach; he
watched the trees and the birds; he slept well in our old room
and tolerated the long ride home without discomfort. He
fought down his emotions a few times, especially on leaving,
and cockily said that the weekend had been "not bad." "I feel
everything is going very well," he commented. The log says
"speech okay; fantastic leg strength."*

*May 15. Carl talked during breakfast for nearly an
hour about the making of motion pictures. His speech was
very good, did not seem to have trouble finding words—during
physical therapy learned to turn himself in bed to both sides—
Dr. Goldman delighted with progress. Chemotherapy works!
We will give next dose on schedule, blood count okay.*

During the next weeks we took him to the movies
once a week, once to the Bronx Botanical Gardens.

*May 21. Two mild seizures, barely noticeable to
others, but clearly felt by Carl. Unable to speak for one minute after seizure, but speech came back and then we went on
as before.*

*May 23. Awakened with speech very poor and
slurry, although he was able to shout angrily, "Oh, I can't
make myself understood." He calmed down and asked what I
thought of his speech today. Answer (by Sharon): "No change,
but slurry today and you take greater time to answer." He said
he was having extreme difficulty finding words and unless he
concentrated intently he would not be able to speak. He
seemed very tired and weary, almost as though he had a seizure in his sleep, because slowly his speech and energy level
improved.*

May 24. Routine day with Danny for company. Pleasant, watched TV all afternoon, in good spirits. One-minute focal seizure, right face and cheek.

May 26. At breakfast, spilled cocoa. Very tired, slept most of morning. Drowsy on awakening, no memory of period before nap. He reverses action of limbs, moves right when he thinks he is moving left. [This observation continues for several days.]

May 28. Very bright all day. Cheerful, planning to have lots of company this week. 8:30 P.M. small motor seizure in right eye region, barely noticeable, but speech much worse after that. Dr. Goldman's orders—keep him quiet. Don't worry about small seizures, they can't be helped. Speech reversal is due to pressure in the brain.

May 30. Lunch visit with friend. Outside on the bench under favorite tree. Speech poor all day. Carl is very depressed. He says he has to "say" phrases to himself several times before he can speak them, which is very tiring for him. This activity is not noticeable to the listener.

May 31. He received the fourth dose of chemotherapy, this time at home. We have lost all hope of a real remission. Looking back on the past six weeks, there was a "good" period of perhaps five days, that's all. Otherwise only the slow progress downward.

May–June 1973

Time was running out on us. My mind, my imagination kept leaping ahead. Like a climber about to start on a dangerous expedition into unknown territory, I went over the terrain, the anticipated possibilities a thousand times in my mind, my dreams.

The thing I was most afraid of during that time was the moment Carl would lose speech. Why, I don't know, but I always pictured it as a particular moment. He would wake up one morning as he had the first time when the arm was gone and now speech would be gone. "The robbers rob you at night." Then he would no longer be able to tell me—it would be entirely in my hands. The thought did not occur to me that, even then, he might still want to live. It seemed inconceivable.

During May and June there were several frightening episodes of choking. A bit of food would become lodged in his throat and he would be unable to expel it. Or some mucus or liquid would go down his windpipe and he'd be unable to cough. The beginning symptoms of a weakness or paralysis of the swallowing apparatus and the cough reflex. For the moment we kept him propped up at a sharp angle in bed and watched his eating and drinking carefully, always ready to intervene. Later, it would mean liquid foods sipped through a straw and still later, suction, to keep him from choking. I remembered a friend who had died from a brain tumor, quickly and mercifully, it had been said. During the last days she hiccoughed uncontrollably. *When* was the state when living became intolerable?

I had a small Siamese kitten once, from the same litter as Rumpel. It was six weeks old and very beautiful and one late evening playing with the other kitten it jumped and fell out the window on the thirteenth floor, where we live. I ran down the stairs and around the building. It was night; it had rained during the day. I did not see the kitten at first and was terribly afraid at what I would see when I did find it. Then I heard a tiny sound, like the peeping of a small bird. There was my kitten, a white round puffy ball on the ground, all intact, no blood, no torn flesh. I picked it up very carefully and it whimpered and rested against my shoulder, where it fainted. I brought it upstairs, phoned vets and animal shelters and was told it was too late at night for emergency care of the kind such a badly injured animal was likely to need. Put it in a box and if it's still alive in the morning, bring it.

I was afraid to look in the box in the morning, but the kitten was alive and moved its head. I took it to the vet, who found that its back was broken in two places and several bones were broken, and thought that there might be internal damage, too. Put it to sleep? Something about the way that kitten had cried for help and waited to faint until help was near had touched me profoundly. "If it wants to live that much, it's got a right to live," I said. The vet thought it would take weeks and would be quite expensive and even at that, he didn't think the kitten could make it. "We owe it a chance," I decided.

Five weeks later the kitten came back to us, wobbly and clumsy, but cheerful. The vet said it was an almost miraculous recovery; a very spunky kitten; he'd never seen anything like it. The only thing wrong with it was that it seemed to have lost its instinctive ability to judge distances—it could not jump with accuracy. He thought it might regain that aptitude as it healed internally, but meanwhile I ought not to let it jump.

How do you keep a tiny kitten from jumping? Simple—you watch it all the time and carry it around most of the time. I did that for a week and the kitten thrived. But I could not entirely keep it from jumping and each time it jumped, it fell. It always misjudged distances and landed short of its goal. Worse, it was always slow in its reflexes. When something moved near it, it did not notice soon enough to move aside. And so, not only did it have many falls, it also got hit by objects near it and got stepped on. One day, the kitten managed to get in the way of a folded shopping cart, dislodging it. The cart fell on top of the kitten and its back was injured again. I remembered picking it up the second time to take it to the vet, almost two months since the first accident, and speaking out what I had learned so slowly: "A handicapped animal really cannot live. Not like a person—it really isn't fit to survive." And Carl, looking at my distraught face, had said gently, "You're not doing it a favor letting it go on like that."

So I took it to the vet and told him to put the kitten to sleep. I cried on the way home. I could not have done it myself.

I carefully read the labels on all the drugs Carl was taking, especially the warnings about overdoses. The descriptions were too gruesome, the horrors worse than those currently experienced. This made no sense. A neighbor died of a heart attack. How I envied him and his widow. . . . Was there any way of inducing a heart attack? High cholesterol foods combined with alcohol combined with tranquilizers? The nurses said a heart attack was painful; a patient could go on for a long time afterward and suffer repeated attacks.

Coma seemed the most wonderful, the most desirable state to achieve. The patient was out of it in a coma—no pain, no consciousness. They kept telling me, it's hell on the relatives, but hell is a relative term and I did not think they knew what they were talking about. With a little bit of luck that might be the way it could go, naturally—and before much more damage was done. But whoever had had a little bit of luck last year? I had no confidence in luck.

It was the end of the school term and I was home all the time. I tried to get out of the house by myself an hour every day and began walking around in the neighborhood, making big circles around ten blocks, making small circles. I avoided the few pleasant streets with their private homes and small neat gardens. I prowled around among the empty lots, the machine shops and warehouses, the litter and ugliness of industrial sites. Still, one day I took a magazine and sat down on a pleasant bench in the neighboring housing projects, under a newly green tree. The shrubbery made a semicircle, sheltering the bench, and there was a bed of iris to look at and since I could not read with any concentration, I looked at the pretty bed of iris. It started me crying; the tears seemed to come readily those days.

"Don't cry," someone said. It was one of two women who had sat down next to me. The one who spoke was a very ugly girl in her twenties, obviously severely retarded. Her hair was cropped short and disheveled, her clothes fitted her awkwardly.

The other woman, possibly an older sister, wore a loose housedress and rolled-down stockings. "What's the matter?" she asked sympathetically and without much curiosity.

"My husband is dying." I began to sob loudly now, suddenly unashamed and unselfconscious.

The retarded girl put her arm around my shoulder and repeated, "Don't cry, don't cry."

"Yah," the other one sighed. "I know . . . Father and mother dead and she's all I've got."

They let me cry and the retarded girl patted my shoulder. I felt at home with them; they wanted no explanations. I was more than half-crazy, those days. . . .

I began seriously to explore my options for terminal care. I could see that if I wanted to keep Carl home much longer, I would need to have a doctor to supervise his care. There was no telling how much longer the weekly visits to Dr. Goldman could continue. Goldman could not possibly take over the function of a GP in attendance, but I felt certain he would cooperate with the doctor I would find. I tried to find a doctor who would promise to make house calls. This turned out to be quite difficult.

My old family doctor turned me down, because he did not think Carl could adequately be cared for at home much longer. He explained it all very persuasively, in terms of the patient's comfort and well-being. "What you're really saying is, you would put him on intravenous and other machines," I insisted.

"Certainly we would want to do what makes him most comfortable at the time," was the equivocal answer.

In an emergency he would make a house call, of course—but with a specialist as the supervising physician, this would present a certain ethical problem. He was not my man.

I tried several others, but apparently no one was anxious to take on such problems. Finally Dr. Bill Rothstein, the resident who had been so helpful and friendly at the beginning, promised to make himself available for house calls whenever I needed him. He also offered to talk to Dr. Goldman about it and to make clear that he would work under his supervision. It was wonderful of him to offer this and it took a load off my mind. As it happened, we never made use of his generosity, but it meant a lot at the time.

Next, I looked into the possibility of nursing home care—just in case it really became impossible for me to carry on. This was an even worse problem. As the social worker had earlier warned me, nobody would accept a terminal case for nursing home care. My only hope was to hospitalize him and of course hospitals had rules against accepting terminal cases, except in emergencies. Very well, if it came to that, it would have to be an emergency. In Carl's condition, emergencies could arise daily.

One of the new nurses questioned me sharply about my decision to keep him home. How long was I going to do it? As long as he is conscious, I answered and maybe later too. She discussed this with me in detail. She approved of keeping him home now, but not if he were to go into a coma. Why not?

"Because if you do, you'll have to move out of the apartment, afterward," she said simply. She knew.

All the others had talked of practical obstacles, which were impressive, but to me seemed simply challenges to be surmounted. The reason she mentioned made sense. I thought about it, long and hard, and made a decision. In making it, I learned that I intended to survive Carl's death. Also that I intended to keep my apartment. All those fantasies and nightmares of suicide and madness were nonsense. I hated myself for the disgusting robustness of my health and the vitality and resilience of my psyche. No matter how I hurt now and how impossible thought of the future seemed, I would do what I had done before; I would survive. I was a survivor from way back.

My mother's sister Margit Neuer, called Manci, was a heavy, strong woman, with blue-black hair and enormous vitality. She was a medical doctor, had married a one-eyed psychiatrist twenty years her senior, divorced him, lived with a succession of lovers, all of them brilliant men with serious flaws of one sort or another. She had worked her way through medical school, living on potatoes and black tea, a chain smoker. After graduation, instead of opening a private practice and finally earning a decent living, as one supposes she might have, she went first into a municipal hospital where she worked with old charity patients; later she worked with crippled children. She and my mother had had a mythical quarrel a year or two after my birth, so they did not see each other for years after. Thus I did not really know her. I heard that the quarrel was about money;

my mother was supposed to have refused Manci money to see her through medical school. Another version of the story was that it concerned a man or perhaps it was a question of their different life-styles—they were both domineering women who could not tolerate interference with whatever it was they strongly wanted at the moment. Manci never set foot in our house for all these years and saw my mother only during the period of their mother's—my grandmother's—terminal illness, which was cancer.

I was seven or eight at the time, and remember horror stories of how the doctor opened up my grandmother's belly, found it full of cancer and simply closed it up again. I saw that vividly, something straight out of Grimm's fairy tales, the wolf calling on the three little pigs, who opened his stomach, filled it with stones and sewed it up again. It seemed to me Grandmother's stomach must be somewhat like that, full of small, slimy stones covered with crawly things one finds under rocks. Grandmother was suffering terribly and my mother came home night after night, crying noisily and passionately, telling everyone all the creepy details of what went on in that hospital. During that time I saw Manci occasionally; she came to the house in her white doctor's coat, her short hair trim and efficient around her face. She never cried, but looked gloomy, heavy-lidded and it seemed to me she suffered more than my mother.

Then came the end and an awesome story, told in whispers by my mother. Manci, who had been one of the doctors attending her mother, usually gave her the evening morphine injection. Things had been very bad and the morphine no longer did anything for the pain. That night, Manci had given her mother a larger dose than usual and so it was all over; her suffering was ended. The story was told in awe and admiration; only a strong woman like Manci could do this. I tried then to picture the scene to myself, but could not. I believed it wholly and do so to this day.

A Death of One's Own

On the day of my grandmother's funeral I remember
having a curious view of the three sisters: my mother
and Manci, both tall, heavy, well-shaped women un-
recognizable in their mourning clothes, and their
younger, crippled sister, Klari, who was hardly as tall as
a teenage girl, standing side by side just before they
went down the stairs to the waiting black cars. All three
of them were weeping, Klari sobbing softly, my mother
with short cries that were almost like speech. Manci
sobbed darkly and terribly, in heaving groans that shook
her broad shoulders. She seemed to me mute, like a
huge animal stricken by some unnamed dread. I had
never seen such grief before and it made me cower in a
corner. Yet I observed the three of them with the re-
lentless curiosity of a bright and well-protected child
and noticed, with astonishment, that for a moment the
two tall women touched each other as though to keep
from falling. It was the only moment of tenderness I
ever saw between them and it frightened me, because I
understood it was coming out of destructive fear and
guilt. I was not allowed to go to the funeral and had the
rest of the day and night to contemplate and relive that
dark, confusing moment. Manci did not come to our
house again; it appears that the quarrel resumed soon
after the mother, who had been a gentle, ineffectual
woman with fluttering hands, had been buried.

As for me, Manci simply disappeared out of my life,
not unlike the dead grandmother, and because, after
that time, my mother hardly spoke of her, it seemed to
me then that there was little difference between one absence and the other. *Partir, c'est mourir un peu*—I remember coming on this phrase in a high-school French
text and feeling a quick stab of recognition. That's how
it was and always had been. The old fear so often reinforced into certainty: absence was dying.

With her mother's death and her own departure,
Manci had for me entered the realm of myth. Whatever
I know of the rest of her life has been pieced together
from secondhand accounts. In 1938, after Hitler occu-

pied Austria, she left for Holland. It was typical of her tremendous vitality that she was one of those who escaped early and by an ingenious and desperate device. Dutch friends, eager to rescue her, found a sympathetic Dutchman willing to enter a *pro forma* marriage with her, which secured her Dutch citizenship. The marriage was soon ended by divorce, but Manci had a few years of relative security. She could not practice medicine, but earned her living as a physiotherapist. She was able in her turn to help secure a residence permit for Mueller, which saved him and her sister Klari for a time at least from the ordeal of living as stateless persons and legal outcasts.

The three of them, sometimes living together and always very close, began again, in middle age, to build a new life in a new place. They had many friends and Manci found another man, a refugee writer and an active Zionist. Then came the Nazi invasion of Holland. Manci's lover went to Palestine; she hoped to join him as soon as possible. Meanwhile, she lived under the constantly increasing restrictions and terror imposed on Jews—nightly curfews, harassment, the wearing of the yellow star. Deportations of Jews began early in 1943, first with the elderly. By then, Dutch Jews had already been herded into ghettos. Manci escaped this by managing to get a favorable classification on the Nazi "exception list." Muellers voluntarily accepted placement on a transport to Budapest. Although she was a Hungarian by birth, Manci could not use this loophole for escape because of her Dutch citizenship. Her friends worked hard to provide her with an immigration permit to Palestine and arrangements were under way to get her there by an underground route. Meanwhile, they secured false identity papers for her and found her a place to stay which she considered safe, the third floor of an old house in the center of Amsterdam.

By that time Jewish transports were leaving the city daily. The Germans had organized this process efficiently and those selected for transport were called up in an orderly fashion, as though they were being drafted. Since street arrests were few, Manci's chances to escape the tightening net seemed quite good. Her new papers identified her as non-Jewish, so that even in the case of an interrogation she might talk her way out. For added security, she had discarded her old identity papers by giving them to a Dutch friend who lived in the same house, asking her to destroy them or hide them securely.

Then her luck ran out. There was a traitor in the underground group in which her friend worked and the house in which Manci lived was raided by the police. No one was interested in her, but the police made a thorough search of the apartment downstairs, which included taking all the books off their shelves. In the process, they discovered Manci's identity papers hidden in one of the books and immediately arrested her, not just as a Jew, but as a criminal involved in illegal activity. She didn't have a chance, after that.

The end of this story came to me in a strange, roundabout way. Long after the end of World War II, when survivor memoirs were being published, there appeared a book by a Dutch woman, telling of her experiences in Amsterdam during the Nazi occupation. The woman had been imprisoned in a Dutch civil jail, which she described in detail. One chapter dealt with a woman nicknamed "Pills." The description fitted Manci, and Dutch friends, who read the book, inquired of the author, who confirmed her identity. These friends then sent the book to surviving relatives; I saw it in translation.

According to that account, Manci spent several months in a regular Dutch jail. As her nickname indicated, she practiced medicine. The woman who wrote about her described her as motherly, strong, supportive. She kept up the morale of all the other prisoners by her jokes, her endless fund of anecdotes, her tough-minded courage. The day she was ordered to get ready for transfer to Westerbork—a transit camp from which transports to the East were assembled—she gave away her few possessions and joked that she had always wanted to travel light. After a few weeks at Westerbork, she was placed on a transport to Auschwitz. One of the women on that transport survived and later told the author of the book what became of "Pills."

She was taken on a train to Auschwitz, in a car full of children. She knew where she was going or guessed it. On arrival at Auschwitz, prisoners were segregated into groups in what was called "the selection." Physically strong people, doctors and those knowledgeable in foreign languages were sent to the labor battalions; children, the weak or sickly, the aged were sent to the crematoria. It is clear that Manci could have saved herself, at least for a time, but she elected to stay with the children from the train and so she died in the ovens of Auschwitz.

Those of us who had escaped tried to do what we could to stay in touch with those "inside," but it was not until some time after the end of the war that we learned of Manci's fate. My mother died and never knew. I do not remember exactly when I found out, but long before I did, Manci had become my nightmarish preoccupation. She, the myth, was alive then—the strong, vital woman I remembered, trapped in the death camps. A few years after I learned of the manner of her dying I began to use her name as my pseudonym in my writing. It was a primitive gesture of sharing the totem of a name with the dead. I could not mourn my aunt personally because I had not really known her, but I always understood that she had died in my place. In the place I should have occupied.

June 1973

Waiting for death
the white corridors lead nowhere.
Sterile air holds nothing. An egg shell
shutting out the busy living.
White core——absence of essence——
suspended breath——
Death will at least be a cracking,
a break——
wind ripping the seamless surface.
A sign——
a mark in the smooth terror
of sand:

We had two trial runs of "emergencies," one late in May, the other the middle of June. One day there was blood in his stool—a symptom which could mean a perforated ulcer or internal bleeding from another cause. When massive doses of steroids are given, internal bleeding is a constant danger of which the doctors had warned us. The amount of steroids Carl was taking— which were essential to keep him functioning—far exceeded established limits. We called the doctor, the hospital. The volunteer ambulance arrived within ten minutes and two husky men placed him on a stretcher and gently carried him out. As they lifted him, it struck me how small and light he had become, how comfortably the narrow ambulance stretcher sheltered him. Everything went so quickly, so smoothly—the ambulance driver made it to the hospital in seven minutes, while I sat beside the stretcher, holding Carl's hand. Let this be it, I hoped—he had no pain now and would lose consciousness gently. Nobody would operate on him. He'd be spared the horrors ahead. I could read his face as he could read mine. We both had the same thought. He closed his eyes. Hurry, I urged the driver on, suddenly filled with the opposite impulse. We must get him to Emergency before there is more bleeding—we must save him. Keep him with us just a little longer. . . .

He was rushed through Emergency and upstairs to Internal Medicine. An internist I did not know had already been alerted by Dr. Goldman. There would be X rays first—meanwhile, I was asked to go to registration and check him in. How many times had I been there already this past year? . . . Still, it was always the same slow filling out of forms. The clerk asked me for a deposit of $240—to cover the first two days. "We have Blue Cross, Major Medical." I explained what was plainly written on the form.

"There is a balance due on your record," he informed me stiffly.

"There must be some mistake. My bill is all paid."

"Your husband cannot be admitted unless you pay the deposit."

"I just brought him by ambulance, an emergency. I didn't bring my checkbook. Besides, I don't owe the hospital anything."

"Our records show plainly—"

"Listen," I shouted. "I paid this goddam hospital over fifty thousand dollars in the last year. My husband carries insurance—what do you want from us? He may be dead up there already, while you're keeping me here with this crap."

The man got up angrily. "He can't get in unless you pay."

"Get me the supervisor. I'll sue you and the hospital and—" Several people came over to me and urged me to sit down.

"Get the supervisor," I raged. "I'm not sitting down— Don't you mess with me. Let everybody hear how you treat people—" I picked up the desk phone and started dialing Dr. Goldman's number.

The clerk came hastily out of a back office. "I just spoke to the supervisor," he said; "it's all right, we'll check him in. You can straighten out the bill tomorrow."

Thanks for nothing. I was trembling with rage and frustration. To have gotten into a physical fight with someone would have been a relief—I suddenly realized I was afraid to go upstairs and find out whatever I would find out. I still had margin left for fear.

But it turned out to be nothing at all, this time. The bleeding had been superficial, probably from some ruptured capillaries—a side effect of the steroids, but a harmless one. Just to make sure, they would keep Carl overnight, then we could go home again.

We both felt so relieved. The next morning's dialogue in the business office was equally unexpected—the supervisor offered me a full and sincere apology. Not only was the bill all paid up, but the hospital owed us money for some drugs which had been ordered and later returned. Further, the clerk had been wrong in acting the way he did in any case—even if I had owed money he should have offered no difficulty over admission in an emergency. . . . And in the future—the supervisor discreetly indicated she knew there would be future admissions—just mention my name as you register and there will be no trouble.

She did it handsomely and was as good as her word. Still, I was not sorry I had made a scene the night before. If they treated me this way, who had paid these huge sums and who could defend myself articulately, what must they be doing to those really unable to pay? . . .

The second emergency was of a similar kind and although the first one had ended so well, this one was just as frightening. With a patient as sick as Carl was, every emergency is terrifying. This time there was no difficulty with admissions. He had to stay several days for tests, which all were negative. He seemed able to tolerate the drugs he was taking amazingly well. The delight he showed each time on coming home made me feel good about our complicated hospital-in-the-home situation. He so much preferred it to being in the hospital, even only for a few days. . . . What was more, these two emergencies had really given me reassurance. I now knew how to beat the hospital rules on "no admission for terminal cases." I knew how to get him admitted in an emergency and I knew there could be one again, at any time. When he needed the hospital, it would be available to him. Only afterward did I realize how desperately worried I had been about this problem of admission.

June 1973

It is difficult to perceive the casual way in which horror piles upon horror. Each day's worsening state slides into consciousness so imperceptibly one doubts one's own judgment. Once in a while, one dares to take a good look—and the depth and quality of change opens up before one's eyes like a pit.

There is no radiance left in him. The monster has even killed his smile. Now, with his sagging face, his drooling lips, the smile has become a grimace, a poor, pathetic imitation of an inward gesture. What he has left is a grin of innocence, a baby's grimace of delight when there is body comfort. Sometimes, rarely, he can still command a twinkle which starts in the eyes and crinkles the corners of eyes and mouth. It comes from deep within him, an inward chuckle.

His speech is a constant struggle against unwilling muscles, lethargic vocal cords, clumsy coordination. He speaks with rocks and mush in his mouth, stumbling over the syllables, swallowing parts of each word, scrambling others. One can read his speech by scanning its score, anticipating the sequence of words like solving an acrostic. The words tumble out of his mouth like hot rocks and pebbles.

June 1973

We were on a roller coaster. On Saturday, June 23, he suddenly could not hear. Earlier that day he had complained of blurring vision and inability to find his place on a line he was reading. That trouble disappeared quickly. But the hearing difficulty continued. Carl explained what he experienced, expressing himself accurately and with great care. In response to my shouted question, "Do you hear me?" he answered, "As though miles away in a tunnel."

A half hour later he could hear loud speech, but only at close range. Still, we took him to a movie, as we had planned, which he seemed to enjoy, although he heard only about half the words.

Sunday his hearing and vision returned to their normal level. Possibly, it was just a sign of general tension and fatigue.

Monday, just as suddenly as the first time, his hearing failed. It seemed almost as though a switch were being turned on and off. A loose connection, flickering on and off. He could still hear when spoken to directly in his left ear, but most other sounds escaped him. Although he seemed otherwise alert, in fact overexcited, he became more and more despondent. I was terrified by what was happening. Was the tumor pressing on the hearing nerve? Nobody had ever mentioned that possibility.

I called Dr. Goldman, who could not explain this new symptom. From the location of the tumor it was impossible that there should be pressure on the auditory nerve. He recommended waiting a few days to see what developed.

I called Dr. Ambrose, who responded to the note of panic in my voice by at length explaining to me why this must be something not connected with the spreading tumor. Frankly, he could not think of an explanation, but then he was no hearing specialist. I had told him that Carl had had a hearing problem for many years, that he was practically deaf in the right ear and had been twice operated on by Dr. Samuel Rosen. He suggested that since the vision difficulties and several other symptoms had appeared and then disappeared, perhaps we were dealing with a passing phenomenon here too. Why not wait a few days? But, with his usual kindness, he suggested I call him back the next day.

Carl seemed very little reassured by my reports of these talks with the doctors. Tuesday the hearing was as bad as the day before. His despondency deepened. To cheer him, I tried giving him the hi-fi earphones and to our pleasure, he could hear the music, although I had to turn the volume up quite high. This diverted him briefly, but his misery and restlessness were too deep for comfort by toys of this kind.

At naptime he could not sleep. Finally, he called me to his bedside. The moment I saw his face, grave and drawn inward, I could feel what was coming. I fussed with the chair, the movable gate on the side of the bed. Ceremoniously, he indicated I might sit on the bed.

Several weeks earlier, when things had still been so much better—how could I imagine how bad things would get in so short a time?—I had been haunted by my usual fantasies of what would happen "later." Obsessed with the fear that I would not understand his needs, that he would not be able to tell me, I had tried clumsily to bring up the subject.

"Why do you struggle so hard?" I had asked. "You make it so hard on yourself. Why not just let go?"

He had pushed his good arm against my chest and with all the strength he could muster, he had shoved me away. His eyes had been cold, angry. "Is that what *you* want?"

"God, no." I truly meant that. "I want to go on as long as you want it. But I must know when—"

"When I cannot speak," he said. "I don't want to go on that way."

That had seemed clear enough. Yet I remembered his earlier statement: "I don't want to live as a cripple." And, "How much more can I suffer? I'm so alive."

Yes, that's what he was, even now—so fully and des-

238

perately alive and suffering so terribly. Now that I felt his despair, I did not want to hear what he would say. All the preparation, the anticipation, the fortifying of myself had not helped at all.

He said it simply. "Enough. I've had it."

I put my head on his chest; that was all I could do.

"You must not cry," he said, speaking quite clearly.

So I stopped crying and tried to brace myself for his next words.

"Help me," he said.

I felt only panic. I did not answer, I could not answer. My cheek touched the warm live skin of his chest; so he had held me and comforted me when I had been troubled and distressed. That was all over. He never again would help me nor help himself. And I was even more entrapped. "Wait," was all I could think of. "Wait. Your hearing may get better, just the way it did the other day." The more I talked the more I began to believe it.

He did not think so. He had lost all hope.

"Forty-eight hours?" I pleaded. "Tomorrow the children are coming. Give yourself some more time to think," I urged. "We can talk about it again."

He agreed and our hands went out to each other. He soon fell asleep. From exhaustion? From relief?

I had stalled for time almost instinctively and now that I had gained it, my panic only mounted. Forty-eight hours and then what? I did not believe in miracles.

Dr. Samuel Rosen is a distinguished ear specialist and surgeon, famous for a surgical procedure he has perfected and with which he has saved thousands of people the world over from loss of hearing. Because of the inordinate demands made on his time and skill, it is very difficult to get an appointment with him. The usual waiting time is three months, but it can be longer.

I called Dr. Rosen's office the next morning at 9:00

A.M. and demanded to get an appointment that day. The receptionist thought I must be crazy and suggested six weeks. I explained it was an emergency. The receptionist suggested taking the patient to the hospital where emergencies could be taken care of. We sparred for quite a while—I was hoping to get to speak to the doctor directly. Finally, I explained the situation exactly—sparing her none of the harsh details. Would she talk to the doctor and perhaps I could call back in half an hour and speak to him? Apparently somewhat stunned, the woman agreed.

Carl's hearing was just as bad as it had been the past two days. I told him of my conversation and elicited the semblance of a smile.

A half hour later the nurse asked if I could bring my husband to Dr. Rosen's office in an hour. Could I? Of course.

No nursing team ever moved as fast as Sharon and I did that morning. Although it usually took an hour and a half to get through dressing and breakfast, we had Carl dressed and ready in half an hour and despite the usual midtown traffic, we were in Dr. Rosen's office with time to spare.

Before he examined Carl, I briefly filled the doctor in on his current medical state and the history of the past year. The examination was soon over. Dr. Rosen spoke to both of us, from time to time speaking directly and close up to Carl.

"There is no evidence that your hearing loss is due to the brain tumor; in fact that is most unlikely. It may be a totally unconnected phenomenon. But with all the drugs you are taking and all that is going on there, it is impossible to find an immediate cause with certainty. There is some function left and the fact that there is this flickering on and off is hopeful. There is really nothing I can do or anyone can do—just hope that it will come back in a few days."

"The nerve of hearing is not paralyzed or destroyed?" I asked.

240

He shrugged. "I don't think so, but it's impossible to tell. It may be just the general pressure caused by the expansion of the tumor."

"But he heard quite well with the earphones. Doesn't that indicate that a hearing aid might help him?"

Dr. Rosen looked at me in astonishment. Mere laymen don't argue with him. He obviously and with some effort made allowances for my hysterical state. "A hearing aid takes time to fit, it is under the best of circumstances difficult to get used to and causes some irritation to the patient until he adjusts to it. It may do absolutely nothing for your husband."

Carl's eyes, attentive and trusting, went from one face to the other. He could not hear us.

"If there is even the slightest chance it may help—"

Dr. Rosen looked at me with sympathy. "Your husband is a dying man," he said softly.

"Of course, but you don't understand. He wanted to kill himself yesterday over this, over not hearing. He's been fighting so bravely—"

"Mrs. Lerner, what difference does it make for the short time he has? It may do nothing at all for him; it may even annoy and irritate him more. It's quite expensive—"

My anger flared. This might be the most famous doctor in the world, but he was talking about one thing and I another. "This man will kill himself if he cannot hear," I insisted. "He's entitled to a chance. The hearing aid will give him a psychological boost, even if it doesn't do anything at all. He'll work at getting used to it, he'll have hope—don't you see?"

"Would you want to get it even if he could only hear for a week or two with it? The pressure may increase . . ."

I looked at him hard. "For a day," I said.

"You're an amazing woman," Dr. Rosen said in a tone of genuine respect. He turned to Carl. "We can try a hearing aid, Mr. Lerner, which may or may not help you. You'll have to work with it for a while to see if it gives you an improvement. At first it may annoy and irritate you. Are you willing to try?"

"Anything," Carl said.

Dr. Rosen now moved briskly. "I think I can help you get it fitted sooner than usual." He went outside and made some calls. A few minutes later he returned. "Can you get your husband to have his fitting done right now?"

I did not even stop to consider the difficulties. "Sure."

He handed me a slip of paper. "I spoke to the man who runs the place. He'll give your husband a temporary set which he can use for the next few days, while the earpiece is being made." Turning to Carl he repeated that and explained that the temporary piece would not work as well as the custom-fitted one, but might give him some improvement. Another week gained by that device, I thought gratefully.

Dr. Rosen shook hands with Carl. "You're a brave man," he said warmly, "and you've got quite a wife. . . ."

Carl responded with his most beautiful smile—like the old days.

In the elevator I first glanced at the slip of paper Dr. Rosen had given me. "My God," I said to Sharon, "do you know where that place is? Forty-second Street and Fifth Avenue. And it's ten minutes to twelve. It's impossible to park there—how will we get Carl out?"

"I'm wearing my uniform," Sharon said, "for just such occasions. You just pull right in front of the place and we'll take him out."

Okay—nothing was impossible—today. The three of us were on a high no drugs could give us.

Ten minutes later I was driving downtown on Fifth Avenue, wedged tightly in four rows of traffic. Traffic on Forty-second was solid and in order to stop in front of the place I'd have to circle two more blocks. I made up my mind quickly. At the intersection, opposite the Forty-second Street library, I brought the car to a stop in the center lane. If I stopped near the curb, we would have no room to take the wheelchair out. Furious honking from behind and beside us. I spied a traffic cop half a block away and figured he'd come over and give us an assist. Sharon and I jumped out, opened the trunk, set up the wheelchair. The honking stopped and under the eyes of all the drivers in the traffic we had totally stalled, we transferred Carl to the wheelchair and he and Sharon proceeded to the hearing aid place. I jumped back in the car, marveling at the forbearance of the much maligned New Yorkers. The traffic cop had never bothered with us at all. We had done it again. . . .

Just to reassure me that the world was still normal, I could not find a parking garage to accept my car on six tries. Finally I managed to park the car some twenty blocks away, grabbed a cab and arrived jittery and upset at the hearing aid place. What I found quickly calmed me: Carl with a hearing aid and a very pleased expression on his face. "It works." He could hear at normal speech level.

The owner of the place gave us a sizable, unasked-for discount and promised to have the custom-made earpiece special-delivered within a week. He warned Carl that there might be fluctuations in his ability to hear with the instrument; sometimes there were hums and interferences. He was a nice man, trying to help as much as he could.

Carl was so buoyed up and excited, he decided to "take a walk" instead of waiting for me to bring the car around.

"It's noon traffic on Forty-second Street," I warned him.

"My old beat," he said happily.

So Sharon wheeled him downtown on Fifth, while I took a cab to the garage. We arranged for a meeting place on the East Side. Carl loved his outing, the crowds, even the attention he was getting.

Driving the car to meet him, I felt as though the most wonderful thing had just happened. Reprieve . . . I realized that without thinking, back there in Dr. Rosen's office, I had acted for Carl, spoken, for once, not out of my fears and grief and pity, but out of that insatiable vitality of his. I had no idea that that was what I would be doing—as Dr. Rosen had indicated, it probably made little sense to anyone but Carl and me. Despite all my agonized anticipation and floundering and preparation, I had voted for life, not death, and won a reprieve. Even for one day . . .

That evening Carl sat by the open window, the hearing aid in place, and looked out over the city. Suddenly, his whole face lit up in surprise and awe, a kind of inner radiance. "Listen . . ." A bird was chirping outside. "I hear . . . better—" His hand flew up in a sweeping gesture.

"Better than before you were sick?" I guessed.

He nodded vigorously, inclining his head to the sound, the new experience.

It was as close as I would ever come to a miracle.

July 1973

During the next two weeks Carl lived in a euphoric state, enchanted with regained and newly discovered sounds. He spent hours listening to records and the radio; he seemed to find new enjoyment in his outings to the garden or the playground where he watched the small children and listened to their chatter. No question that the miracle of his restored hearing had renewed his zest for living. He was all smiles and grins and displayed almost irrepressible good humor.

Still, his general condition was much worse. The side effects of chemotherapy were daily becoming more uncomfortable. The skin erosions were spreading and deepening. It required frequent tedious treatments of tinctures, powder and heat to keep the condition somewhat stable. The skin simply did not seem capable of healing. As a result, not only his daily care was more cumbersome and unpleasant for him, but he suffered serious discomfort, even pain, in sitting in one position for any length of time.

A tiny cut on his toe became infected and quickly grew worse. Toe, foot and leg began to swell and we had to use frequent hot soaks and heavy doses of antibiotics to cure what normally would be a negligible injury. Toward the end of the month, there were ominous changes in his blood picture. Chemotherapy was becoming more and more risky.

On the other hand, his deterioration progressed with greater rapidity. Speech was getting worse all the time. He struggled for each word, brought out one or two syllables in slurred speech, had to repeat these in hopes of dragging out the next syllable or word by sheer rhythmic momentum. Sometimes this worked; some-

247

times it did not. When the word or whatever part of it there was going to be was all there, it hung heavily, with obscene bulk between us, something musty and ill-defined, odd, bulging syllables protruding so that I might, from them, guess the shape of the whole. Fortunately, I have always liked word games. I guessed right perhaps half of the time. If I did, he proceeded. If I did not, there was the sharp, angry waving of his hand. For a man as neat and precise in his work habits as Carl had always been, this vagueness must have been a particular torture. Sometimes, when he failed to communicate he might try another tack. It got so we let one or two words stand for entire sentences. Or else I helped out by asking several leading questions or by reshaping his half-pronounced lead words into entire statements. Then he would signal assent or disagreement by look or gesture. It served well enough for ordinary conversation.

There were episodes of memory loss and inappropriate behavior, sometimes paradoxically coinciding with the ability to speak surprisingly long sentences. In the middle of July Carl suddenly popped out with: "How can I move this leg [pointing to his good leg] without getting the other one in the way?"

"What do you mean?"

"Walk. I should be able to walk with crutches." He went on to express, quite clearly, that he wanted to be more independent and felt quite strong enough to walk. Apparently he had forgotten his actual condition.

When it was pointed out to him that his right side was paralyzed and that that was the reason he could not walk on crutches, he said cheerfully, "Well, I'm wrong again."

At another time he was unable to count to seven and could not remember the simple rules of a children's game we were playing. Five minutes later he remembered the name of an obscure plant none of us could remember. . . .

During the first week of July blood tests showed a dangerously low platelet count. In view of that Dr.

July 1973

Goldman decided to discontinue chemotherapy. His main argument was that he did not think the drugs had had any effect on the advance of the disease in the last month, but that the side effects were becoming so serious and unpleasant that the treatment should be stopped. I did not disagree. It was obvious we were running out of time and out of miracles. I was beaten down, lethargic and very, very tired.

Five days after the chemotherapy was stopped, the blood count improved and there was obvious improvement in the skin condition. The positive effect on Carl's well-being and comfort was so great, I felt reassured we had taken the right decision. A few days later, his range of activity was almost as great as it had been a month earlier—he could sit comfortably for long periods of time, enjoyed long walks in the wheelchair. However, his enjoyment of company grew less and less as the speech difficulties increased.

July 13, 1973

His mental function has been greatly impaired. There are incidents of childish behavior—decorating the table and floor with prune pits and grinning about it; unable to decide on whether to use the spoon or fork for mashed vegetables; inability to make the simplest choices, such as which shirt to wear. He cannot deal with abstract ideas, subjective or future tense, conjectures. He can deal with here and now, the immediate, the visible and with simple recollections of the past. Remember this or that person? This or that happening? His behavior seems to me appropriate to a charming, bright and cheerful six-year-old. His anger, when thwarted or delayed in any of the gratifications of his needs, spurts up uncontrollably. He does not reason, does not seem to hear or comprehend explanations.

His memory is gone, except for a certain narrow field. He remembers his work, most of the people he knows

*well. But the book I am reading to him chapter by chap-
ter, and which he goes through the motions of "reading"
himself, leaves no imprint. He loves it while it is being
read to him, but is unable from day to day to remember
what we have read the day before. [The book we were
reading during that time, incidentally, was Dr. Rosen's
autobiography, which he had beautifully inscribed to
Carl.]*

When Carl had a problem more profound than one
relating to his physical comfort, he signaled it by agitation and restlessness. His frustration was obvious and
painful to watch. I tried to encourage him to communicate with me, one way or another.

We had one such "talk" on the fifteenth of July.
The way we "conversed" was that I guessed various sentences he might want to say, offering him a choice. He
selected the right one by a gesture or a "yes" and "no,"
and we would go on from there. It was quite an adequate means of communication for people who were
well attuned to each other. But I was acutely conscious
of not wanting to "give him ideas," to state things for
him. I did not want to give him clues he might misinter-
pret. Especially since, as it turned out, I obviously mis-
interpreted much of his state in my daily observations.

"You're feeling bad about something? What?" He
could not say it. He had never asked about the next
chemotherapy and so I had not told him we had
stopped it. It would have been just another discouraging
bit of information. I was careful not to allude to that
topic. "Are you feeling worse? Does anything new hurt
you?"

That was not it, either. He gestured toward his
mouth.

"You're feeling bad about your speech?" That was it,
of course.

He struggled and brought out: "Terrible."

"I want to understand what you experience. Do you
think in words?"

He made several tries and finally managed:
"Assolully."

"Whole sentences?"

Yes. We developed that theme. It appeared that he
knew exactly what he wanted to say, stumbled over the
first word and then, even if that word was understood,
forgot the rest of the sentence in the struggle over the
next word.

I was stunned by the lucidity of his explanation. His
mind was functioning at a much higher level than ap-
pearances made one believe. What the nurses and I had
interpreted as impaired mental function was merely a
function of his impaired communications network. He
could express himself only in the most primitive terms
of grammar and vocabulary, presenting us with a picture of "pseudoretardation." For behind it all, his
thought was as sharp and keen as ever. How he must
suffer. . . .

Meanwhile, he seemed pleased and relieved at having
explained this much.

It was strange, but sitting beside his bedside, holding
his hand and talking to him—no matter how pitiful our
means of communication—everything seemed good
and peaceful to me. There was a kind of happiness in
these moments, these parts of hours, unlike any before.
I knew without thinking that there would never be anything like it again and that everything was worth it, all
the horror and agony and long slow suffering of those
months was as nothing against those moments of total
peace and communion. All my fears about stages, one
more terrible than the other, about definite cutoff
points, crippling, loss of speech—all these fears had
nothing to do with the process we were experiencing,
that gentle transformation into acceptance of the inevitable. I understood something then, which I would
need in the coming weeks: there would never be a point
as long as he was alive that it would not be that way
between us. We had come a long way together in life;
we were going as long a way together in dying as two
people can.

I wanted very much to try and tell him that, but I did not know how. "I will miss you," I said, tears filling my eyes.

He nodded gravely and brought my fingers to his lips. "You—go on . . ."

"I won't know how," I said, "but I'll try."

We sat still for a long time.

"You'll know," he said finally, firmly and clearly. Then he closed his eyes and, serenely and in full relaxation, fell asleep.

The next week passed, quickly and terribly. During all of June and most of July he had watched the Watergate hearings on TV. No matter how bad his state, he always seemed interested in that spectacle and was able to follow the testimony with understanding and alert interest. Now, as his general ability to comprehend slowed down, he also lost interest in TV. His attention span shortened, while sleeping and drowsiness took up more of his hours. Speech got so bad he was incomprehensible for days. He gave up trying, sometimes laughed at the absurdity of his efforts to bring out a word, sometimes simply "turned off."

Wild things happened. One night the hearing aid irritated his ear, but Carl would not remove it, apparently anxious about shutting himself off further from his surroundings. When I finally convinced him to take the earpiece out while he was sleeping, it turned out that he heard perfectly well without it. At another time he suddenly seemed to be gaining in leg strength. He could stand on both legs, with support, something he had been unable to do for months. Incomprehensible phenomena—almost as though some crazy spirit were having his fun turning switches on and off at random. . . .

Since his attention span was now so short, I tried to divert him by giving him paper and crayons. To my surprise, he took them up eagerly and drew a figure, which he indicated was himself. It was a charming, wobbly figure, appropriate for the drawing of a four-year-old. He did not seem to realize that the arms were missing; that head and body were totally out of proportion. I then asked him to write a word, any word he could think of. He could not choose. I said, "Write 'hot.' " He did: "HOS." I asked him to pronounce it and he said "hot." He was similarly unable to write "yes," which he spelled "yee" and pronounced "yes." For the first time, he was unable to write his name, but did not seem aware of it. The activity amused and pleased him. My breath choked inside me—how far down had we come. . . .

I was by then so accustomed to the roller coaster on which we were riding that setbacks, no matter how disastrous, did not discourage me. They might be offset, the next day, by some spectacular, irrelevant gain. I was determined to keep on working on our communication system—if for no other reason than to have something by which both of us could be challenged.

A friend of ours, a film editor like Carl, suggested that I might try to make flash cards to which Carl could point to indicate his needs. I decided to try it with a single word on each card. Choosing the most urgent demands he must communicate for his daily care, I made cards for juice, milk, blanket, BM, urinal, too hot, too cold. Then I made a 3 × 5 card with the words "I want" on them and showed him how to combine the two. I laid the cards out on his bedside table, expecting him to point. To my amazement, he immediately pronounced "I want" perfectly clearly, then proceeded to say the other words in a sentence. In one sitting he went through the whole repertory: "I want milk; I want blanket," etc.

Delighted with this response, I made cards with simple action phrases: "to go out"; "to see TV"; "to move" etc. Carl did almost as well with those as with the single words, but I had to pronounce the words for him first, showing him the card. Once he had pronounced them after me, he seemed to be able to read them with ease and to say them clearly. There were a few words he could not pronounce, such as "I feel fine," but he could say, "I am fine." "Music" was impossible, but "records" was spoken clearly. Apparently, the missing memory of a word can be prodded by visual and oral stimuli. Once aroused, pronunciation is possible, where previously only babbling sounds were made. Fascinating and very useful. Carl's care was much simplified by the use of these flash cards. He began at once, and with enthusiasm, to use them, combine them and pronounce them. When that was too difficult or when he was tired, he pointed to them. The success of this system and its obvious utility made him happy.

The weekend of July 28–29 he was more than usually quiet and thoughtful. He managed to say a few sentences with the flash cards appropriate to his care, but otherwise made hardly any effort to speak. Old friends came to see him and he sat quietly with them, quickly growing tired. I made a notation in the log Sunday evening: "Seems disgusted with trying. Seemed 'strange' to me all day, but I cannot specify how." He sat trapped in his silence.

When I came into his room early Monday morning, he looked grave. He indicated he wanted to speak to me. I sat down by his bed.

He struggled for words and I tried to help him, by going through the routine questions. None of that.

"Nothing that's on the cards," I said. "You have something else on your mind?"

He nodded eagerly. Immediately, I felt fear. I wanted to escape. It was as though I could read his thoughts. I shifted ground. "How do you feel?"

An angry wave of his hand.

"It's not so bad," I said in response to his unspoken sentence. "We can still talk."

He did not think so. Something in the deliberateness of his gestures, his stern expression, conveyed it to me long before we could find the words. There was no use trying to run from it. He had made up his mind to die.

"What do you think?" he asked me without the words ever having been spoken.

I refused to answer. I told him he could not ask me to make that decision. It was his to make. I could not take the responsibility.

That made him impatient. He knew all that, why repeat it?

"Because you keep asking me," I said. "I want you to stay with me as long as you can. As long as you want. You're not a burden. Even if you were, I can take it. I don't ever want you to make the decision on account of me. I can hold out as long as it takes." I tried to touch him, but he would not let me. What I really wanted to say is, I need you, but I felt I really had no right to put that on him. I did not want him to live for me any more than I wanted him not to live in order to spare me. In our stumbling and impaired language I wanted to give him the autonomy he always had had as a whole and healthy man.

He heard me differently. I was saying the wrong words. His mouth moved, his lips and vocal cords struggled. It took a long long time, and an effort which must have taken much of his failing strength. Finally he brought out the one word. "How?"

God, he was long past me. He really meant it.

"I can't do it," I said miserably. "I can't kill you. I can't even help you to do it. I'm sorry. I couldn't go on living if I did."

He squeezed my hand. He understood. He really understood. I felt suddenly so much lighter.

I explained carefully that the only way was to follow the advice of several doctors I had consulted in anticipation of this question. He could refuse medication; he had every right to do so. If and when he did, I would uphold him; the doctors would accept his decision; no one would interfere. Three doctors separately had assured me that, considering the huge doses of steroids he had been taking for so long, stopping them suddenly would put him into a coma within twenty-four to seventy-two hours. What I did not tell him was that they had also said stopping the steroids might bring on a grand mal seizure which would, most likely, put him into a coma or kill him instantly.

He understood and reached for my hand.

In a rush of panic I begged him to wait. "We can still communicate. Give yourself more time, you might change your mind."

He looked at me, holding my gaze firmly. Then he closed his eyes. Right now there was no more need for words. We sat like that, his hand warm and live in mine, in a kind of enchanted circle of silence and assent. Very calm now, with a serenity that comes when there is nothing more to expect and nothing more to fear.

Suddenly he spoke with his old voice, very clearly and cleanly. "Ger-da. Gerda."

He did not usually call me by name. It alarmed me. "What's wrong?"

He managed a full sentence now, clearly and without hesitation. "Just wanted to know if I can still say it."

Much later, thinking about it, I understood what a tremendous effort speaking those words must have taken. At the time, it simply threw me. I felt as though his strong, sensitive fingers had touched a spring deep inside me, pressed ever so gently, and now everything, all my feelings, the pain, the love, the terrible grief lay open. I put my head on his chest and he drew me nearer with his good hand. This once, we cried together.

The next hours, all day, there was a wonderful aura of serenity around us. We both understood it was "given" time. Time added as a gift. There was no need to speak, everything was quite clear between us. He awoke the following morning. He mumbled and fumbled with words I could not understand. His request seemed to have some urgency. Finally, I could make it out. He wanted to be taken to our bed, the large bed in our room.

It was the hour, the single, precious, risky hour when we were alone in the apartment. I had recently salvaged it out of our institutional existence by sending the night nurse home one hour before the day nurse arrived. It meant much to me to know that there was one such hour left each day.

I'll never know how I managed to transfer him from his bed to the wheelchair and, without assistance, from the wheelchair to our bed. It had been many weeks since I had last been able to manage a transfer without the assistance of another person. The bed was far too low for easy transfer and I was sure I would not be able to get him out of it, once I had him in it. Anyway, I managed. I settled him in comfortably, raising up his head with propped pillows, secured him against falling out and rolling off. Then I slipped in beside him on his "good" left side. I held his hand. Eyes closed, it felt normal, right. It felt like the hundreds of nights we had lain together side by side. Thirty-three years. A whole lifetime.

We made love that morning. It was sad and sweet and tender. He did what he could and gave me all his gentle love, his strength and secure trust in himself and in both of us, despite his helpless and crippled body. Amazingly, he spoke to me with his body the way he had always spoken. For the final thirty days of his life he would never again trust himself to let me come that close again. It was his way of saying good-bye, while he still could function with some wholeness. A man giving up his love by loving. That's the way he wanted it. That's the way he went.

August 1–

August 26, 1973

IN THE HOUSE OF THE DYING

In the house of the dying
the windows stand wide.   Dry
air, still as mid-day, pauses.
The heartbeat waits.
Stark shadows of tree trunks
push iron bars into the chamber,
flicker.   Pulse, once and
again.   Harsh and rasping
an intake of breath.

In the house of the dying
pale vapor shrouds sound.   Everything
has been said before.   There is
nothing new left.   Whatever is,
is all there is.   Strangling breath
pushes through the rock bed
of all there was.   In the dusty
waiting the pulse persists,
fluttering, captive.

In the house of the dead
the light has turned stone.
One can touch time, frozen.
Ashen pallor streaked with steel
bands.   A small wind stirs.   Softly,
dry dust swirls over cheeks, hair,
bone.   There is no more.   Only
the painful light.

He had made up his mind to die and he had made his decision rationally, freely. After all my planning and scheming and agonizing he took yet another decision out of my hands by insisting on going to the hospital. He could not do it at home, he said or indicated, and I know he did not want to be at home because he wanted to spare us, the children and me. Also, because what he had to do was very difficult and probably, truly, it was too difficult in the rooms he loved and where life kept pulling at him with a thousand associations and reminders.

Dr. Goldman arranged to admit Carl to the hospital for steroid withdrawal and made him promise to take his medicine until he was actually admitted. He did not want any complications to occur at home. Deliberately and with faintly ironic amusement, Carl heard me explain that it might take a few days before he could get admitted to the hospital. Would he agree to go on as usual? . . .

He understood, thought about it. Okay, he indicated, smiling his old beautiful smile. It was a characteristic, true moment. I have never loved him more than I did then. His formidable quiet courage, his sense of humor, his concern for others. His love of life—he managed to die with love of life.

He was serene the next three days. At the time I thought I would always remember these last days in every detail, but they have faded out of memory as have so many of the most painful times. I remember wheeling his chair to the dinner table, then pouring milk in his glass and saying to myself, It's the last time he will be here. It's the last time I will stand by the sink washing the dishes and see his face. The last time. I thought, It's the way it is in the movies, the last twenty-four hours of the condemned man. The last meal.

I remember that and I remember it feeling unreal even while it happened. Then, saying to myself, Stop it, you can't pull it that way. And going through much of that time with everything shut out, making my gestures and thoughts normal. We kept to our regular routine. I read him a bedtime story, held his hand for a while before he went to sleep. Yes, I sat in the room by his bed in the dark and the monstrous refrain kept coming back. Still, I slept that night. We both slept in our separate rooms that last time in our house together.

Nothing is better than ignorance of the future. August 1, a Wednesday morning—and no word from the hospital. Carl was very upset and restless and tried hard to convey it to me. As though there were anything I could do about it. . . . One moment, sitting by the phone, the wild absurdity of it came through to me. A man had made up his mind to die, but he must wait because there is no room at the hospital. No room at the inn.

The phone call finally came in the early afternoon. I called the ambulance and the transfer was made very swiftly. Carl kept his eyes half-closed and seemed relieved to be going. He was placed in the beautiful corner room in which he had been once before. At 6:00 P.M. he formally refused the life-essential medication.

From the moment Carl entered the hospital his serenity and attitude of patient resignation returned. He wanted no music, no TV. He wanted no visitors except the children. Sometimes, he let me read to him. Mostly, he simply lay there, waiting.

Death by illness, like birth, is possible only with the participation of the individual. This consists both of a release—letting go—and an active advance—goal-directedness. The patient must at one time or another seek death—as a release, as sleep, as the end of pain—before physical destruction can end life. He must release his hold on life and surrender himself to nature. This is the process of dying.

Nature is cruel and dying is cruel, either by being too swift or too slow. The body has to be destroyed and the will to live has to be destroyed and the two are not the same. Usually, sickness takes care of the body and pain destroys the will to live. But in certain sicknesses where physical destruction is irreversible, but where there is no pain, there is an ambivalence, a conflict of opposing impulses. This psychological agony is perhaps worse than pain. That was Carl's case.

For him the process of letting go took many weeks. I had thought of it in rational terms as a single decision which needed to be made and to be carried through or allowed to be carried through by nature or active intervention. It was rather a wavelike movement with peaks and troughs, advances and retreats and very few plateaus. The body, attacked so overwhelmingly in its nerve center, the brain, responded by rallying its every resource and fighting back fiercely, long beyond hope or sense and in the face of his rational determination to die. The psyche—itself a complex system of contending emotions, patterned behavior, past history, memories and instincts—wavered even at the end, alternately hanging on and letting go.

It is impossible and probably futile to analyze this process and yet, in an effort at understanding it, I feel compelled to do so. While I myself was in it, a struggling, aching part of it, the need for comprehending what was happening was my only means of "distancing" myself, however badly I succeeded. The journal, the log, the diary, the poems all together reassured me of my roots in life, of my ability to stay out of the process sufficiently to survive. For all along a dark and terrible urge pulled me toward a total acceptance and sharing of his experience. I cannot say I ever wanted to die with him, rather it was that I felt I *was* dying with him and must save myself somehow. Why this was so I do not know.

The ambivalence and complexities Carl experienced were reflected in my own contradictory emotions. For months I had been prepared for his death, as well as one ever can be. There was hardly a night I did not wake up from dreaming his death in one way or another. Yet in the last terrible twenty-four hours, when I sat by his side when he lay unconscious with 107.8 fever and ice-cold, purple limbs, as hour after hour he struggled for each breath, I found myself thinking with the utmost concentration—praying—Stop, give up—die, will you? But the several times when his breath actually stopped, for twenty or thirty seconds, I prayed equally fervently, Come on, breathe, just once more, breathe! And when the painful rattling intake of air occurred I breathed too and for a few seconds let go of my tension.

It was because life was so strong in him—unable to swallow, he had had no food in seventeen days; according to everything medical science knows, he should have been in a deep coma three weeks earlier. But he kept on sending consciousness into that room, the spirit, the mind, the brain—half of it already taken over by the cancer—that brain somewhere still having enough of everything left so he could be whole and his eyes could speak.

So, despite his courage and resolution, it was in the end a slow, natural process. For the terrible eighteen months of his illness I had struggled to help him to die his own death—in the sense in which Rilke speaks of it—his own death, not mine. That meant separating myself from him, separating my survivor-need for death, my guilty longing for working out all those neglected past deaths, from what he needed. And what he needed was to live, as fully and totally as his body permitted, and when that was gone, to live some more. And only when at last I understood that—without the words that I had always needed in order to understand anything at all—when at last I understood that profound elemental connection he had to life and which was and could not be mine—I could let go.

He said good-bye so many different ways. To his son in one long serious conversation, quite early, during the first week after chemotherapy had been discontinued. I

had thought to shield him from the knowledge that the
last hope of postponement was gone, and he never
asked when chemotherapy would be resumed. I thought
his failing memory had made him lose track of the
weeks, but when I learned about his talk with Danny, I
knew he was, once again, way ahead of me. He told
Danny very simply and straight he could not live totally
helpless and that he was thinking of me and of him
when he said this. He wanted nothing to be done to
prolong his life when the time came. Then he changed
the subject and talked about politics.

His farewell to friends: sometimes an embrace held
just a trifle longer, a handshake with a deep, meaningful
look. To the nurses who came visiting in the hospital—
Al, Alan—a special smile and handshake. He said good-
bye to the river, the park, the children, the street where
we lived and the small yard enclosed by the seven buildings which had bounded his freedom for over a year, he
said good-bye to it all at once on Sunday, July 29. It was
a hot evening and Jane and I had taken him out for the
second time that day, a special treat. He sat quietly by
the river holding my hand and watching the sun set
over the hazy skyline and a few slow tugboats passing by
on the river. He wanted, very suddenly, to return home
and refused to be taken on the circular walk around the
playground, which was his daily "outing." We thought
he was·tired, but he had made up his mind already, although he had not yet told me, and he could not bear
to look any longer. That night, on the way to the elevator, he saw a neighbor and refused to respond to his
greeting. He just sat there, withdrawn into himself. The
next night, when we offered to drive him to the park
again, he refused.

He did the same thing, two weeks later in the hospital. Danny was wheeling him to the solarium, but he
tugged at Danny's sleeve and indicated with various unmistakable signals that he wanted to be taken downstairs. It was all queer and wild, for he had checked
himself in two weeks earlier to die; he had not taken any
medication and the coma he had been waiting for re-

fused to come. He felt sicker and worse than ever, but here he was demanding to be taken to the greenhouse. We had to get a pass to take him downstairs and the whole procession of us—Danny, Jane, he and I—went down the elevator and to the other building. I kept thinking it was a procession and it really was. The greenhouse was closed, so we went to the tiny park with its water fountain, stone benches and specimen trees in cement pots. It is a pathetic little park, surrounded by the roar of the tunnel and highway traffic, but a park is a park. He sat still for five or ten minutes, a soft, relaxed look on his face. Then, with the same impatience he had shown that Sunday by the river, he insisted on going upstairs. At once. He never came outside of his room again.

His sweetest, most giving farewell was to Stephanie. He was then supposedly semicomatose, heavily drugged with morphine. Stephanie and I sat by his bed and he opened his eyes. Stephanie had been holding his hand and he now detached it from hers. Slowly, gently, like a blind person, he touched the outlines of her face with his fingertips, her chin, her nose, her lips. Finally he put his hand back into hers and closed his eyes. The gesture brought tears to her eyes and to mine, it was so delicate and exquisite and it seemed to spring from an assured knowledge of what she most needed. It was a perfect gift. The thought passed through me, Why did he not do this for me? but it gave way at once. I understood that he did not have the strength to go through this more than once for each person, each place. He found what was right for each of us; more he could not do. And he had already said farewell to me. I could accept that and so I could let him go. I think he knew it and so, finally, he could also let go.

Carl died on August 26, 1973.

The ending I have just written is not untrue, nor is it quite true. As everything memory serves up, it is a slice of the truth, a layer, a segment.

There is another ending, the nightmare version. It recurs frequently, somewhat like this:

Everything as in the previous version, until he goes to the hospital. He carries through his resolution, he refuses the medicine. He waits for coma, for death. Then things go wrong.

Nothing happens as predicted. Without steroids, the tumor takes over, the sickness progresses by leaps and bounds. Having lost all ability to speak, he now loses the ability to swallow. Choking and gagging make eating by mouth impossible. He can take water, drop by drop; we measure it carefully, coax it down. He chokes on even a drop of water. We give it to him every half hour, suction his mouth, his windpipe. The sickness progresses.

The decision earlier made, the promise not to use machines, means this: standing by his bedside helpless and watching the drop-by-drop nourishment; the choking, the suctioning, the choking. It means saying no the comfort of intravenous feeding. No, no, NO, and sticking to it.

No loss of consiousness, no coma. The eyes stay open and speak. And now there is pain, wracking headaches, fever, chills.

It means saying no to antibiotics, to oxygen tents. There is only morphine against the pain, some sort of drug sleep instead of coma. An easing at least, a loss of knowing for him.

It means staying on guard night and day, speaking for him now that he can no longer speak, saying no, NO and yes, please, yes.

The choking still wakes me, the hot dry breath forced through lifeless passages.

He wanted to die but his body would not give up. I promised to help him and I did by saying no. Watching this struggle, this agonizing reluctant passage, I kept the contract we had made thirty-three years ago with each other. As my father kept the contract, as Mueller did. I kept the contract; more cannot be required.

This is no more true or untrue than the first version. Everything happened sometime. There is yet another ending—untidy, without heroes.

He loved living so much he never could learn to die, even when he wanted it. He was too alive, too strong in body and spirit to give up to the invading monster. As my mother was, who took four years.

No, it was not I who killed him nor did he kill himself. A brain tumor killed him, and if nothing whatever had been done for him, no surgery, no drugs, no painkillers, no suction, he would have died just the same, only more brutally, more hideously. He was trapped, he was doomed. Nature is cruel and indifferent. Death is a random, inevitable disaster.

That is true. And because we, men, women, children, lovers of one another, loving friends, must live our lives in the shadow of death, in the acceptance of this truth, we must try to transcend it. By fighting it off while we can, by dying our own death in our own time, by experiencing the deaths of others as fearlessly and as feelingly as we can. Death is not heroic, it is not kind. We share it and learn it and discover that it is—like life, because it is the other side of life—untidy, mixed up, tormented, transcendent. And accept it finally, because we must. Because we are human.